Texas Range Plants

NUMBER THIRTEEN:

THE W.L. MOODY, JR., NATURAL HISTORY SERIES

TEXAS RANGE PLANTS

Stephan L. Hatch
and
Jennifer Pluhar

with new illustrations by
Keith Westover

Texas A&M University Press
College Station

Hatch, Stephan L., 1945-
     Texas range plants / Stephan L. Hatch and Jennifer Pluhar : with
new illustrations by Keith Westover.
          p. cm. -- (W.L. Moody, Jr., natural history series)
     Includes bibliographical references and index.
     ISBN 0-89096-538-2 (cloth); 0-89096-521-8 (paper)
     1. Range plants--Texas--Identification. I. Pluhar, Jennifer,
1959-   . II. Title. III. Series.
QK188.H38 1993
581.6'09764'09153--dc20   92-5073
                                                                   CIP

Dedicated to:

John Vallentine and Don Ryerson

who sparked our initial interests

in range plants

CONTENTS

ACKNOWLEDGMENTS

We thank and acknowledge:

Keith Westover, for the new illustrations of many of the grasses, forbs, and shrubs.

Lucile Gould Bridges and Texas A&M University Press, for permission to use illustrations from the following publications: F.W. Gould *Grasses of Southwestern United States* (1951), F.W. Gould and T.W. Box *Grasses of the Texas Coastal Bend* (1965), F.W. Gould *Common Texas Grasses* (1978), and F.W. Gould and R.B. Shaw *Grass Systematics* (1983).

University of Arizona Press, for permission to use Lucretia B. Hamilton illustrations from F.W. Gould *Grasses of Southwestern United States* (1951, 1973 copyright by Arizona Board of Regents).

U.S. Department of Agriculture, for illustrations from A.S. Hitchcock *Manual of the Grasses of the United States* (1951), Leithead et al. *100 Native Forage Grasses in 11 Southern States* (1976), *Range Plant Handbook* (1937), and B.I. Judd *Principal Forage Plants of Southwestern Ranges* (1962).

U.S. Department of Interior, for illustrations from C.H. Wasser *Ecology and Culture of Selected Species Useful in Revegetating Disturbed Lands in the West* (1982).

Winrock International, for permission to use illustrations from S.L. Hatch et al. *The Grasses of the National Range Research Station, Kiboko (Kenya)* (1984).

William F. Mahler, for use of illustration in K.N. Gandhi and R.D. Thomas *Asteraceae of Louisiana* (1989).

University of Nebraska Press, for permission to use illustrations from J. Stubbendieck et al. *North American Range Plants* (1982).

Tammy Sanford, for secretarial and technical assistance.

Stanley Jones, Gretchen Jones, and J.K. Wipff, for editing this manuscript.

Shayne Hatch, for assisting in data acquisition.

Patricia Wilson and Raelene Nixon, for technical assistance.

Our appreciation is extended to Nora Lee Hatch and Darwin Pluhar and our family members for their patience and encouragement throughout the preparation of this manuscript.

Texas Range Plants

INTRODUCTION

This book is written to help range ecologists, soil conservationists, amateur botanists, land appraisers, college students, 4-H members and leaders, FFA students and instructors, and rangeland managers identify important Texas range plants. This book describes and illustrates 140 grasses, forbs, shrubs, and trees of economic importance on Texas rangelands. These plants were selected because of their important forage characteristics, poisonous attributes, or their "weedy" or aggressive nature. Species included in this book are from the 4-H's "Master Plant List for Texas Range and Pasture Plant Identification Contests" and "State FFA (Future Farmers of America) Range and Pasture Judging Contest" lists. These two lists have been developed over the years as a result of several individuals and committees.

Each species is described in detail and depicted with a line drawing. Line drawings of each plant show the characteristics necessary for identification. Common and scientific names for both species and family, longevity, season (cool or warm), origin, economic value to wildlife and livestock are given for each species. Following the classification catagories there are a few italicized sentences that describe the plant in non technical terms, give additional common names, and/or folklore uses for the species when known. Finally floral, vegetative, growth characteristics, and habitat are listed for each plant. Recent synonyms for scientific names are included in the text. For a more complete synonymy see S.L. Hatch, K.N. Gandhi, and L.E. Brown *Checklist of the Vascular Plants of Texas*, Texas Agriculture Experiment Station, MP 1655 (1990). Additionally, a complete glossary for technical terminology is included.

Grasses (Poaceae family), described first, are recognized as having linear leaves with parallel venation, nodes and elongated internodes, split or open leaf sheaths, somewhat rounded stems, and inconspicuous flowers enclosed in spikelets. Grasses are organized by the tribe, genus, and species in alphabetical order. The second group described is the legumes (Fabaceae family) which is organized alphabetically by genus and species. This family is recognizable by their pinnately or palmately compound leaves, stipules, and its most common flower type (papalionaceous). The last part of the book is an alphabetical arrangement of other families with the genera and species arranged alphabetically within the family.

NOTE AND WARNING: Information about American Indian and pioneer uses contained herein is for educational purposes and interest. This information was gathered from several sources and is not personal knowledge. It is emphasized that *you should not use the plants for these folklore purposes.*

VEGETATIONAL AREAS OF TEXAS

Ten vegetation areas, or natural regions, of Texas can be defined on the basis of the interaction of geology, soils, physiography, and climate F.W. Gould, G.O. Hoffman, and C.A. Rechenthin, *Vegetational Areas of Texas*, Texas Agriculture Experiment Station, Leaflet 492 (1960). These vegetative areas (Figure 1) set the stage for a wide array of land uses that vary from intensive cropland agriculture, to extensive ranching, to urban development. For a summary of the physical and climatic characteristics of the vegetational areas of Texas, see Table 1.

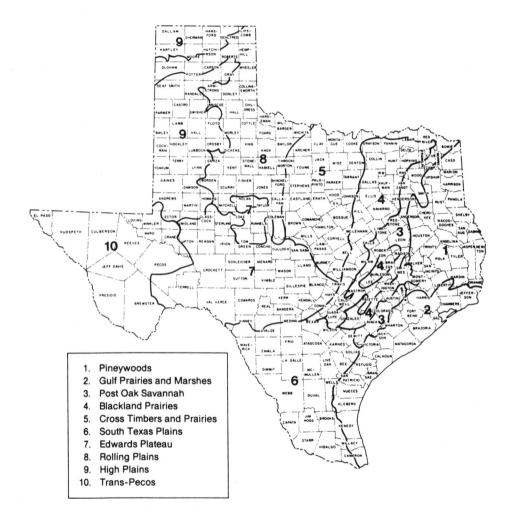

Figure 1. Vegetational Areas of Texas.

1. Pineywoods
2. Gulf Prairies and Marshes
3. Post Oak Savannah
4. Blackland Prairies
5. Cross Timbers and Prairies
6. South Texas Plains
7. Edwards Plateau
8. Rolling Plains
9. High Plains
10. Trans-Pecos

Table 1. Summary of the physical and climatic characteristics of the vegetational areas of Texas. *

	Million acres (million hectares)	Annual percipitation (inches)	Frost-free days	Topography	Elevation (feet)	Major soil orders	Month of peak precipitation (secondary peak)
1. Pineywoods	15.80 (6.4)	40-56	235-265	Nearly level to gently undulating	50-700	Ultisols, Alfisols	Even distribution
2. Gulf Prairies and Marshes	10.0 (4.1)	26-56	245-320	Nearly level	0-250	Vertisols, Entisols	September (May)
3. Post Oak Savannah	6.85 (2.8)	30-45	235-280	Nearly level to gently rolling	300-800	Alfisols, Vertisols, Ultisols	May (September)
4. Blackland Prairies	12.6 (5.1)	30-45	230-280	Nearly level to rolling	250-700	Vertisols, Alfisols	May (September)
5. Cross Timbers and Prairies	15.3 (6.2)	25-35	230-280	Gently rolling	500-1500	Mollisols, Alfisols	May (September)
6. South Texas Plains	20.9 (8.5)	18-30	260-340	Nearly level to rolling	0-1000	Mollisols, Vertisols, Alfisols, Entisols	September (May)
7. Edwards Plateau	25.45 (10.3)	12-32	220-260	Deeply dissected hilly, stony plain	1200-3000	Entisols, Mollisols, Alfisols	May (September)
8. Rolling Plains	24.0 (9.7)	18-28	185-235	Nearly level to rolling	1000-3000	Mainly Mollisols, secondarily Alfisols	May (September)
9. High Plains	19.4 (7.9)	14-21	180-220	Nearly level high plateau	3000-4500	Alfisols, Mollisols	May (September)
10. Trans-Pecos	17.95 (7.3)	8-18	220-245	Mountain ranges, rough, rocky land, flat basins and plateaus	2500-8751	Aridisols, Entisols, Mollisols	July, August, September (November)

* C.L. Godfrey, C.R. Carter, and G.S. McKee, *Land resources areas of Texas*, Texas Agricultural Experiment Station, Bulletin 1070 (1977).

RANGE PLANT CLASSIFICATION

TAXONOMIC CLASSIFICATION

Taxonomic classification is based on morphological, cytological, anatomical, biochemical, and ecological characteristics of plants. These characters are used to group plants into taxonomic ranks (categories), based on similarities or having characters in common. Variation in the classification of genera and species, as used in this book, varies somewhat from the older books. As new information is obtained about a plant group (e.g. species) it may become necessary to change the classification of that group of organisms. Taxonomy is no different than any other part of science, when new information is learned, changes in classification result. For our purposes the classification is within the realm of the taxonomist. However identification, one of the basic processes of plant taxonomy, is important to most individuals. The characters used for identifications should be based on plant morphology rather than non-morphological characters.

Identification is the matching of an unknown with a known identity. This process may include the use of diagnostic keys and comparisons with herbarium specimens or botanical descriptions, line drawings or photographs. Magnification will aide in matching minute details used in keys and visual comparisons. If an unknown matches with a known, an identification has been made. The application of a plant name with these characters completes this process.

For our purposes the ranks used in this book will include: family, tribe, genus, species, and variety. The grass treatment includes all of these ranks. For many people the species will be the rank of most importance. Scientific names (species names) consist of three parts, genus, specific epithet, and authority(ies). The genus is capitalized and underlined or italicized showing that it a foreign word. The specific epithet is not capitalized but underlined or italicized like the genus name. Following the scientific name is the name or abbreviation of the person or persons who described the species. An example is *Panicum virgatum* L. (switchgrass). This species was described by Carl Linnaeus and is indicated by the abbreviation L. for Linnaeus. When scientific names are changed because of a reclassification the name(s) of the people making the new combination follow the name(s) of the original authority(ies) and the original authority(ies) is placed in parenthesis. An example is *Tridens flavus* (L.) Hitchc. This species was originally described by Linnaeus in the genus *Poa*. Later A.S. Hitchcock transferred this name to *Tridens*.

LONGEVITY (Life Span)

Most plants are classified as either annual, biennial, or perennial. Annuals complete their life cycle in one season or one year and biennials in two years while perennials grow for three or more seasons. Annual plants may be either grasses or forbs. Perennials may be grasses, forbs, or woody plants. Most perennial grasses and forbs produce stems and leaves each year from their rootstock or crown. Woody perennials are evergreen or deciduous but do not die back to the ground after freezing weather. These plants grow from terminal buds which produce new stems and leaves. Axillary buds are initiated under certain conditions.

SEASON (Season of Growth)

Cool season plants make all or most of their growth in the fall, winter, or spring of the year. Warm season plants make most of their growth in the summer and fall of the year. Evergreen plants grow throughout the year. Most plants of southern and western Texas grow throughout the year. These plants are moisture dependent rather than truly cool or warm season species.

ORIGIN (Native or Introduced)

Most plants discussed in this book are native to North America. Many plants have been intentionally introduced into North America as forage or ornamental species; others were accidently introduced and have become naturalized, some as pernicious weeds.

ECONOMIC VALUE

The value of a plant species for wildlife (deer, antelope, turkey, quail, and dove) is based on palatability, nutritive quality, and volume. While any particular plant may be of high value for one species, such as deer, it may be poor for another. The highest rating was selected for the plant reported herein. A good rating means it is highly valuable to one or more of the animal species. Fair wildlife rating means it is of average value based on the combined values for volume, production, and palatability. Plants rated as poor are the least valued species because of low values for two or more of the criteria.

It should be noted that the value of a plant for wildlife does not include potential wildlife uses such as nesting cover or loafing cover. Some plant species are very important to wildlife although they are not cosumed as a food source. In fact, some plant species are critical to habitat requirements for a particular species of wildlife but are not food sources, thus they do not appear important in the "economic value" of the plant as addressed in this book. These values are assigned in accordance with the aforementioned 4-H and FFA plant lists as used in competition. It should also be noted that the wildlife species considered here are not all inclusive and do not include potential uses of the plant by non-game species such as songbirds.

The value of a plant species for livestock is determined by its potential forage production, palatability, and nutritive quality. Good ratings reflect comparatively high values for these criteria. Fair ratings are given to plants of intermediate production, palatability, and nutritive quality for livestock. Poor ratings reflect low production, low nutritive quality, or slight palatability. These changes may change for a particular plant depending upon the composition of the plant community present, the geographic location, the particular location of the plant within a range site, the soil type, specific climatic characteristics, animal species, and age of animal. In short, these values vary widely across the state of Texas. The values chosen for the plants represent the most common economic value associated with the plant as a food source for livestock.

Some of the plants are rated as "poisonous" while also being rated "good", "fair", or "poor". This results because a plant may be toxic during one stage of its growth or to a single animal species, or to all animals. Toxic plants may reduce animal growth rates, cause deformities, or cause death. These same plants may be good forage for other animal species, or at least during certain seasons. Detailed information regarding poisonous plants is available from several sources such as E.M. Schmutz *Plants that Poison*, Northland Press (1979).

GRASS MORPHOLOGY

THE GRASS PLANT

The grass family (Poaceae) is composed of highly evolved monocotyledonous plants, which is distantly related to the sedge (Cyperaceae), rush (Juncaceae), and lily (Liliaceae) families. Grasses are typically herbaceous except for *Arundinaria gigantea* (giant cane), a native bamboo species, and are of perennial or annual longevity. The grass plant consists of roots, culms, leaves, and inflorescences of small flowers borne in spikelets (Figure 2). Characteristics and variation found within each of these structures will be discussed separately.

VEGETATIVE PARTS

The root system in grasses, as in most monocotyledons, is fibrous. The primary root system, developed from the embryo, is short lived and persists only until the plant is established. A secondary root system develops soon after seed germination and eventually supports the plant. Secondary roots are developed from the lower culm nodes and are referred to as adventitious roots. In many grasses, when the culm is decumbent or prostrate, roots will arise from nodes that contact the soil. Branching of roots occurs at irregular intervals and not at nodes as does branching of the culm.

The grass culm is generally smooth and cylindrical with in most grasses, enlarged ("swollen") nodes. Leaves, branches, axillary buds, and adventitious roots are borne at the nodes. Grass culm internodes are solid, semisolid, or hollow. The terminal (apical) meristem and intercalary meristems at the base of the internodes account for the growth of the culm as a result of cell division, elongation, and differentiation.

Vegetative reproduction can occur in the grass plant for many reasons, such as culm modifications. Tiller (suckers) are subterranean or ground-level lateral shoots that are erect and usually associated with a caespitose (bunchgrass) habit. Rhizomes (Figure 2B) are underground stems having leaves that are reduced to scales. In addition roots may arise from their nodes. Generally the internode of a rhizome is greatly shortened compared with that of the above-ground culm. Stolons (runners) (Figure 2C) spread horizontally along the ground surface and can initiate a "new plant" at a node by developing roots and an erect culm. Leaves at the nodes may either resemble erect culm leaves or be reduced to scales. Plants that reproduce vegetatively are typically either stoloniferous or rhizomatous except *Cynodon dactylon*, which has both rhizomes and stolons. Depending on environmental conditions, a rhizomatous stem axis may become stoloniferous at the ground surface, or a stolon may become subterranean and rhizomatous (Figure 2D).

Grass leaves occur in two ranks, or rows, and are alternately arranged on the culm. Nearly all leaves are differentiated into three parts; sheath, ligule, and blade (Figure 2A). The sheath is attached just below the culm node and ascends, typically, clasping the internode. Margins of the sheath are generally free to the base although in some genera, the margins are fused, forming a tubular structure, or are fused along the lower margin. Leaf blades are typically flat and elongated. However, many species that have evolved under arid conditions and have folded or involute leaves, an adaptation that reduces the loss of water due to transpiration. Dermal appendages on the sheath and blade vary from smooth, without visible hairs, to densely pilose or hispid. The ligule (Figure 2E), typically present (except in most *Echinochloa* species), is a membrane, a ciliate membrane, or a ring of hairs on the adaxial surface at the junction of the sheath and blade. Figure 8 depicts differences in ligule type, shape, and margin. Auricles (Figure 2E) are membranous projections of tissue present on some grasses on either side of the leaf, at the apex of the sheath, or at the base of the blade.

The prophyll, the first leaf of a lateral branch, provides some protection to the developing branch in its early stages. Typically short and membranous, the prophyll consists only a sheath. The prophyll develops with its dorsal surface fitted tightly against the culm axis and its margins folded over the axillary meristem or base of the branch. The prophyll has two prominent veins and has often been compared to the palea of the spikelet and the coleoptile of the embryo.

INFLORESCENCE TYPES

Grass inflorescences (Figures 3-5) are delimited by the uppermost leaf or portion thereof. By our definition, multiple inflorescences can occur on a single culm. We have used the grass inflorescence terminology of spike, spicate raceme, raceme, and panicle in the traditional sense. Other terms are used for specialized panicle inflorescences. The spike, spicate raceme, and raceme inflorescences have no branches arising from the central axis (rachis). The spikelets are either attached directly or are individually pedicelled (or stalked) upon the central axis. The panicle inflorescence has branches that arise from the nodes of the central axis. Spikelets are seldom borne on the central axis (rachis). A spicate raceme (Figures 3B and 5A) has an unbranched central axis (rachis) with sessile spikelets and short pedicellate spikelets at each node. Raceme inflorescences (Figure 3C) have pedicels that support single spikelets attached to the central axis. Panicle inflorescences (Figure 3D, 4, and 5B-D) can have only primary branches or primary branches that branch and rebranch and have several spikelets supported by each branch or branchlet. By definition, the central axis of a panicle is not a rachis. The rachis is only the axis of a spike, spicate raceme, or raceme.

A panicle of spicate primary unilateral branches (Figure 4) is a common modification of the grass inflorescence. Branches that develop from the nodes of the central axis of the inflorescence are called primary branches. Spikelets on this inflorescence type are racemose (subsessile or sessile) on the primary branch and make the branch appear spike-like, hence the term "spicate." The spikelets are attached along one side of the branch and give the branch a unilateral or one-sided appearance. Paniclees with spicate primary unilateral branches may be described by the arrangement of the branches by using modifiers such as alternate (Figure 4A), digitate (Figure 4B), subdigitate (Figure 4C), or verticillate (Figure 4D).

A panicle of racemose branches (Figure 5B-D) is a specialized inflorescence composed of both sessile and pedicellate spikelets at each node. This condition, found in the Andropogoneae tribe, is repeated at all nodes of the inflorescence except at the terminal node, where one sessile and two pedicellate spikelets are normal. The inflorescence types in this category are panicle of subdigitate racemose branches (Figure 5B), panicle of alternate racemose branches (Figure 5C), and an open panicle (Figure 5D).

SPIKELET PARTS

The grass spikelet (Figure 6) is the basic unit of the grass inflorescence. Understanding the variation in spikelet structure is essential in using this book. Spikelets typically consist of a pair of glumes with one or more florets and the associated rachilla. Florets consist of a lemma, palea, floral axis, and "grass flower" (lodicules, pistil, and stamen) or some portion thereof (Figure 6). Determining where the spikelet disarticulates (breaks apart) at maturity is often important. Spikelets disarticulate from the pedicel, below the glumes (at the spikelet base), or above the glumes and between the florets. Spikelets from four of the common tribes found in the area are illustrated in Figure 7.

Glumes are empty bracts occurring at the base of the spikelet, and their presence delimits or defines the spikelet. Most spikelets have two glumes that may vary in relative size, texture, presence or absence of awns, and several other characters. Some taxa may lack one (such as many species in the Paniceae tribe) or both (as in species of the Oryzeae tribe) of the glumes. When lacking, the lowermost (first) glume is more likely to be absent than is the second glume. Glumes are typically odd-nerved (1, 3, 5, etc., to as many as 13 nerves = veins), and the nerves may extend into awns.

The floret consists of two bracts, the lemma and the palea, which protect the grass flower. The lemma is attached to the rachilla and in many species partly conceals or completely encloses the palea. The lemma typically has an odd number of nerves, which may extend from the tissue to form an awn or a mucro. Commonly only the midvein extends into an awn although all the nerves may extend, as in *Enneapogon*. The palea and grass flower are attached to the floral axis. This very short axis arises from the rachilla and is adaxial to the lemma. The palea is an even-nerved bract, typically shorter than the lemma, lighter in texture, and usually awnless. The palea is adaxial to the grass flower and protects the developing flower parts from moisture loss or extreme temperatures. In the Paniceae and Andropogoneae tribes, the palea of the lower floret is typically reduced or absent.

The florets may be perfect, imperfect, sterile, or reduced (Figures 6-7). A reduced floret can consist of a lemma and palea or can be reduced to one to several awnlike structures. The position of the fertile floret(s) is an important taxonomic character in distinguishing between tribes. In the Paniceae and Andropogoneae tribes, the sterile floret is below the fertile floret. In the Chlorideae, Eragrosteae, Pappophoreae, Poeae, and Triticeae tribes, the sterile florets are above the fertile florets or absent. The Aristideae and Stipeae tribes have a single perfect floret.

The fruit of most grasses is a caryopsis, a hard, single-seeded dry indehiscent fruit in which the pericarp is fused to the seedcoat. Exceptions occur in a few genera such as *Sporobolus*, in which the fruit is an achene and the pericarp is not fused to the seedcoat.

FORB AND WOODY PLANT MORPHOLOGY

Forbs are herbaceous plants that must renew growth from the plant crown on a yearly basis or germinate each year from seed. These plants generally have showy flowers, leaves with netted venation, and herbaceous stems. Woody plants (trees and shrubs) have solid stems due to secondary growth (in width) of the vascular cambium. Figures 9-21 depict many morphological features of the forbs and woody plants described in this book. For more information refer to the glossary. These definitions will help in understanding unfamiliar morphological characteristics in the plant descriptions.

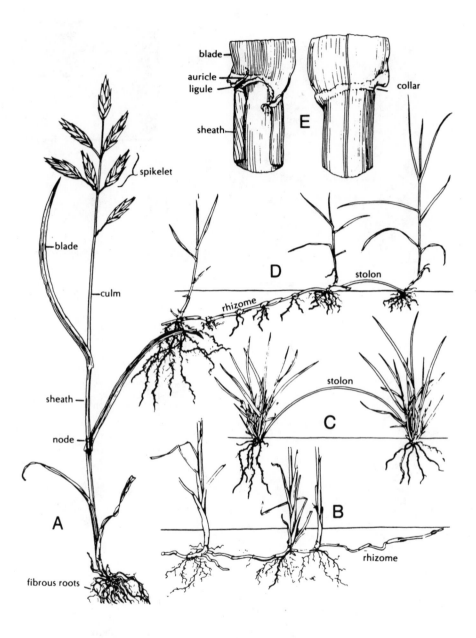

Figure 2. The grass plant (from Gould, 1951): (A) general habit of *Bromus unioloides* (rescuegrass); (B) rhizomes; (C) stolon of *Hilaria belangeri* (curly mesquite); (D) rhizomes and stolon combination in *Cynodon dactylon* (bermudagrass); and (E) junction of blade and sheath; left, adaxial surface; right, abaxial surface.

Texas Range Plants

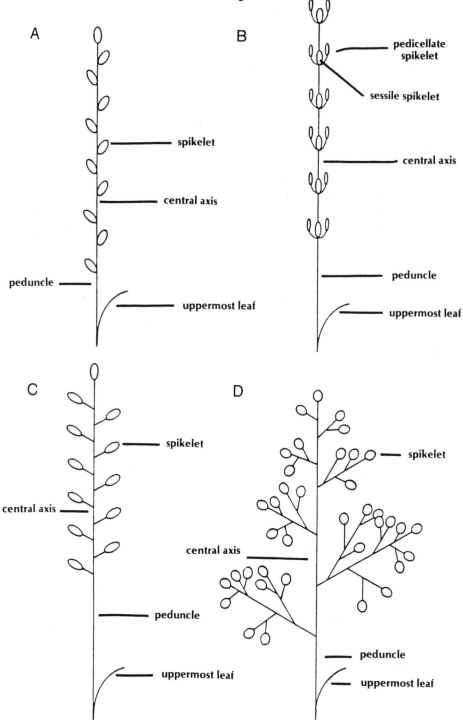

Figure 3. Diagramatic representation of grass inflorescence types: (A) spike; (B) spicate raceme; (C) raceme; and (D) open panicle

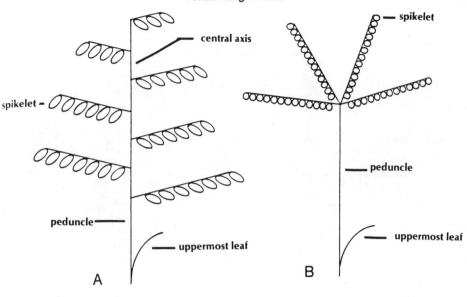

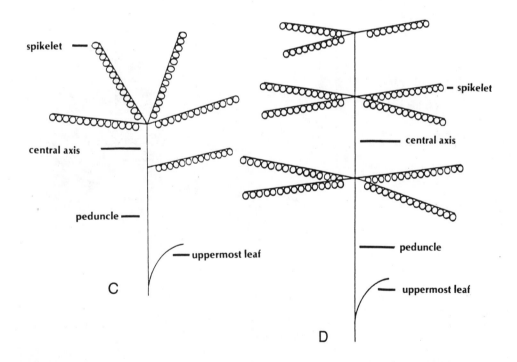

Figure 4. Diagramatic representation of specialized panicle inflorescences: (A) panicle of alternate spicate primary unilateral branches; (B) panicle of digitate spicate primary unilateral branches; (C) panicle of subdigitate primary unilateral branches; and (D) panicle of verticillate spicate primary unilateral branches.

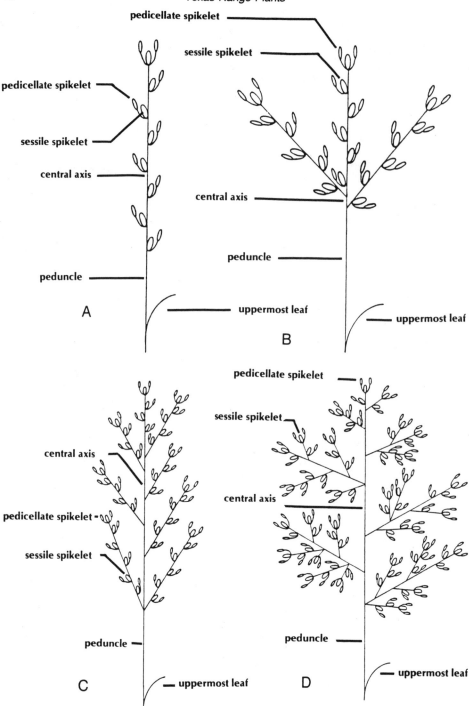

Figure 5.   Diagramatic representation of Andropogoneae inflorescences having paired spikelets at each node: (A) spicate raceme; (B) panicle of subdigitate racemose branches; (C) panicle of generally alternate branches; and (D) open panicle.

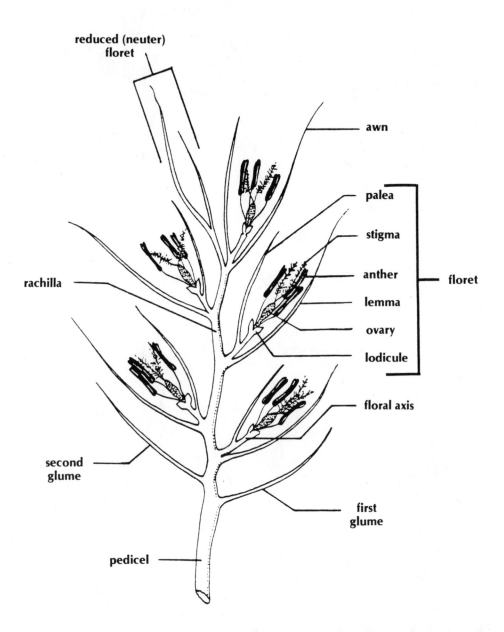

Figure 6. Spikelet parts. Diagramatic representation of a *Bromus* (brome) spikelet with six florets (adapted from Gould and Shaw, 1983).

Texas Range Plants

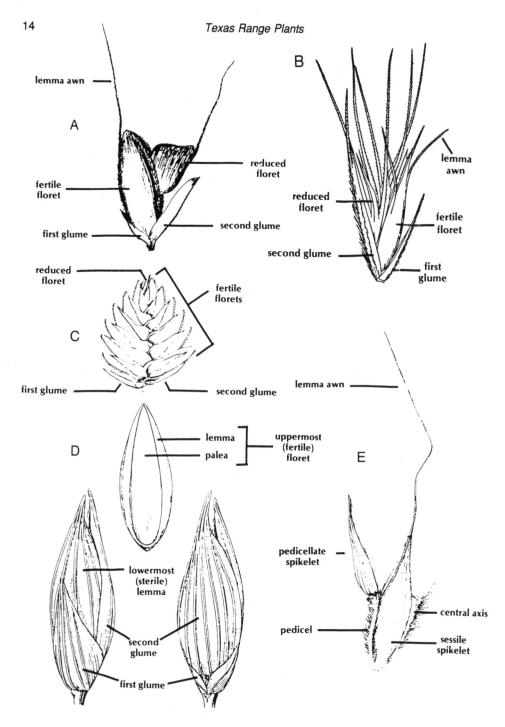

Figure 7. Spikelets representing some genera and tribes found in the State. Species shown may not be found in Texas: (A) spikelet of *Chloris subdolichostachya* (Chlorideae) (from Gould and Box, 1965); (B) spikelet of *Bouteloua rigidiseta* (Chlorideae) (from Hitchcock, 1951); (C) spikelet of *Eragrostis superba* (Eragrosteae) (from Hatch et al., 1984); (D) spikelet of *Panicum harvardii* (Paniceae) (from Hitchcock, 1951); and (E) spikelet of *Cymbopogon caesius* (Andropogoneae) (from Hatch et al., 1984).

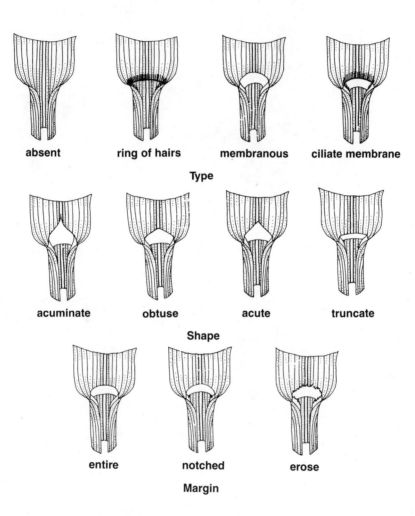

Figure 8. Ligules of grass leaves.

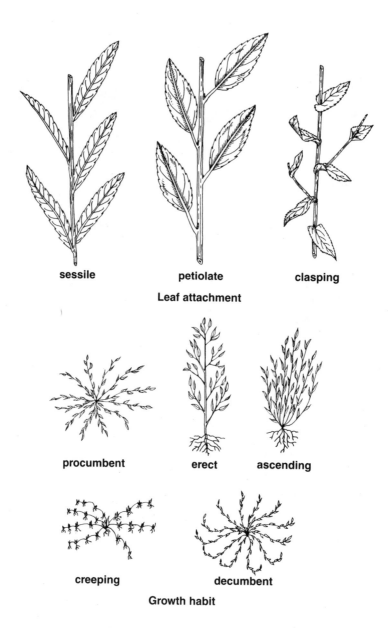

sessile　　　　petiolate　　　　clasping

Leaf attachment

procumbent　　　erect　　　ascending

creeping　　　　decumbent

Growth habit

Figure 9.　Leaf attachment and plant growth habit.

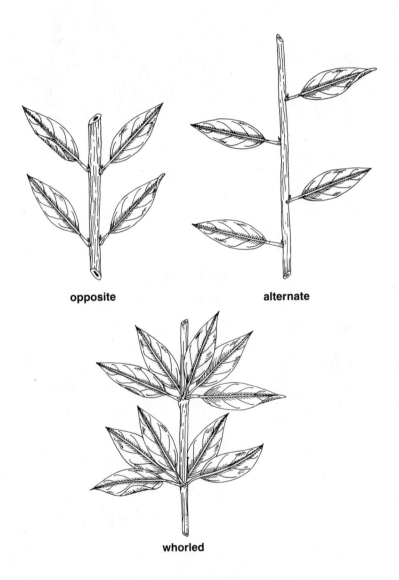

opposite   alternate

whorled

Figure 10.   Leaf arrangement.

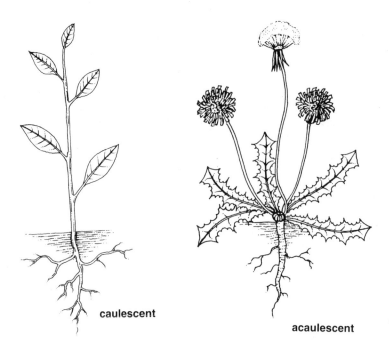

caulescent

acaulescent

Types of forb

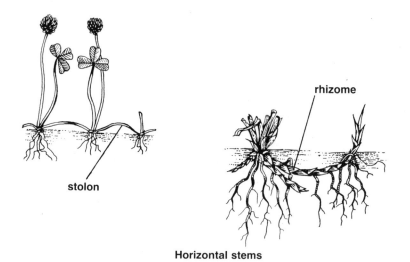

stolon

rhizome

Horizontal stems

Figure 11.   Type of forb and horizontal stems.

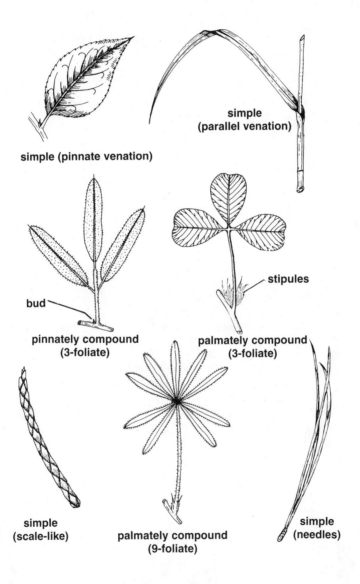

simple (pinnate venation)

simple
(parallel venation)

bud

pinnately compound
(3-foliate)

stipules

palmately compound
(3-foliate)

simple
(scale-like)

palmately compound
(9-foliate)

simple
(needles)

Figure 12.   Leaf types.

Texas Range Plants

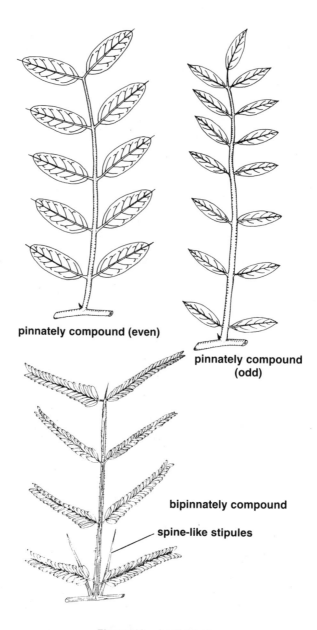

pinnately compound (even)

pinnately compound
(odd)

bipinnately compound

spine-like stipules

Figure 13.   Leaf types.

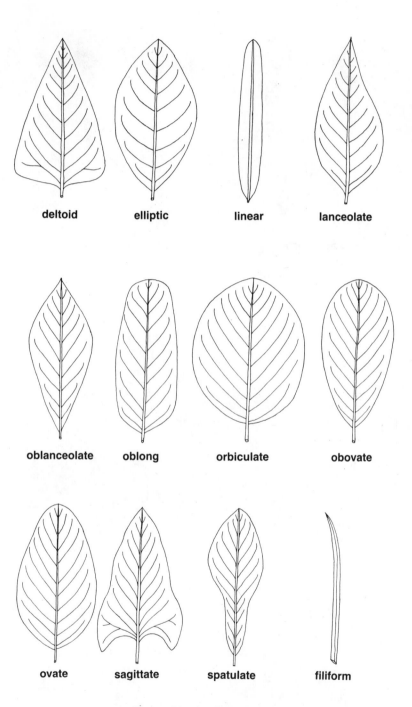

Figure 14.   Leaf shapes.

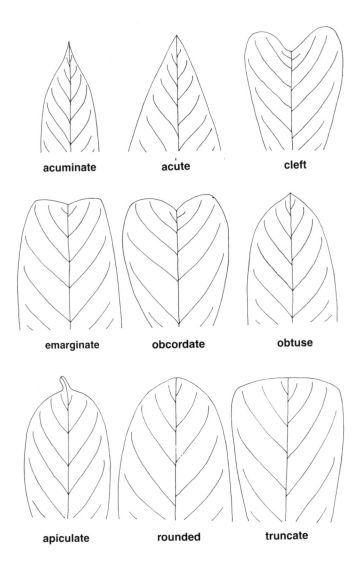

Figure 15. Leaf apices.

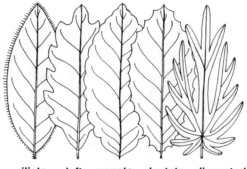

ciliate   cleft   crenate   dentate   dissected

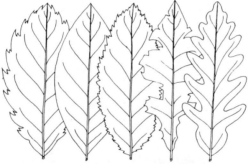

double serrate   entire   erose   incised   lobed

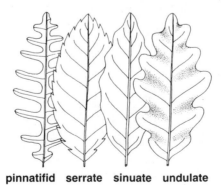

pinnatifid   serrate   sinuate   undulate

Figure 16.   Leaf margins.

Texas Range Plants

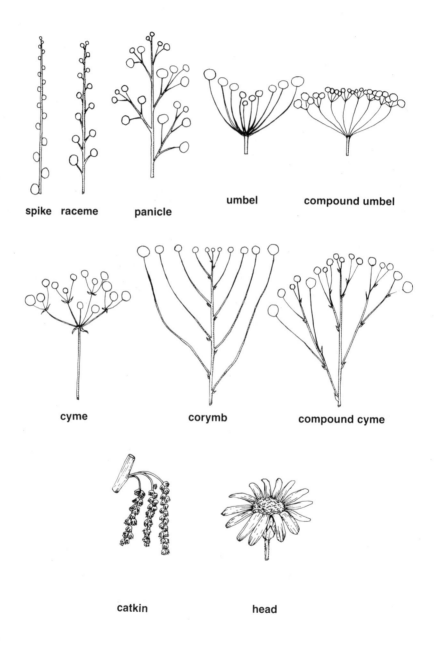

spike   raceme   panicle   umbel   compound umbel

cyme   corymb   compound cyme

catkin   head

Figure 17.   Inflorescence types.

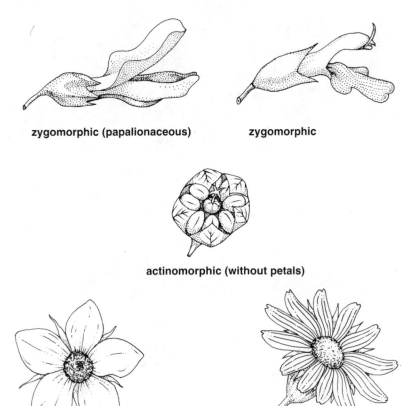

zygomorphic (papalionaceous)   zygomorphic

actinomorphic (without petals)

actinomorphic (with petals)   head (inflorescence
type not a single flower)

Figure 18.   Flower types.

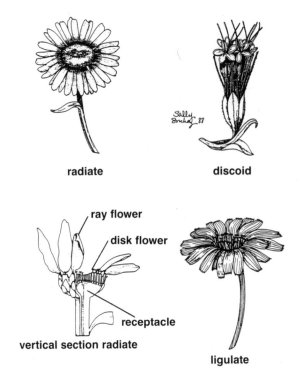

radiate   discoid

ray flower

disk flower

receptacle

vertical section radiate

ligulate

Figure 19.   Asteraceae head types and parts.
             (from Gandhi and Thomas, 1989)

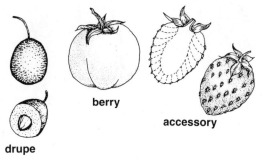

drupe

berry

accessory

Fleshy

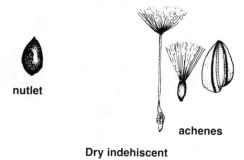

nutlet

achenes

Dry indehiscent

Figure 20.   Fruit types.

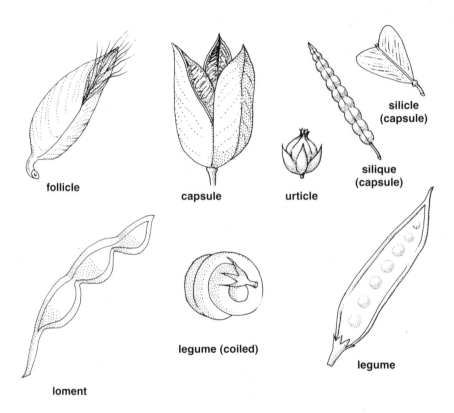

follicle

capsule

urticle

silicle
(capsule)

silique
(capsule)

loment

legume (coiled)

legume

Figure 21.   Dry dehiscent fruits.

PLANT DESCRIPTIONS
AND ILLUSTRATIONS

Distichlis spicata var. *stricta*
island saltgrass
(Gould and Box, 1965)

INLAND SALTGRASS

Grass Family (Poaceae: Aeluropodeae)

LATIN NAME:	*Distichlis spicata* (L.) Green var. *stricta* (Torr.) Beetle
LONGEVITY:	Perennial
SEASON:	Warm
ORIGIN:	Native
ECONOMIC VALUE:	Wildlife - poor Livestock - fair

A strongly rhizomatous grass that characterizes saline sites. The leaves are relatively short, less than 10 cm (4 in) long, conspicuously two-ranked, and numerous along the length of the stem. Male and female plants grow separately but seedheads appear identical. Inland saltgrass becomes straw-colored with maturity.

FLORAL CHARACTERISTICS:

Inflorescence: panicle 2-7 cm (3/4-2 3/4 in) long, contracted

Spikelets: florets 5-9, spikelet 0.6-1.0 cm (1/4-3/8 in) long; lemma 3-6 mm (1/8-1/4 in) long, acute, margins yellow; palea 2-nerved, soft

Awns: glumes, lemmas, and paleas awnless

Glumes: unequal, acute, glabrous, 3 to 9-nerved

Other: plants dioecious, staminate inflorescences straw-colored, pistillate inflorescences green

VEGETATIVE CHARACTERISTICS:

Culms: decumbent to erect, 10-45 cm (4-18 in) tall, numerous nodes; extensive creeping rhizomes

Leaves: basal and cauline; sheaths overlapping; blades conspicuously 2-ranked (distichous), flat to involute, to 10 cm (4 in) long, tapering from the base

Ligules: ciliate membrane, 0.5 mm (less than 1/32 in) long, truncate

GROWTH CHARACTERISTICS:

plants dioecious; starts growth in March to April, when sufficient moisture is available and remains green until fall; reproduces by seeds, tillers, and rhizomes

HABITAT:

margins of saline lakes, ponds and waterways; saline and alkaline soils. Texas distribution: Areas 7-10

Andropogon gerardii
big bluestem
(Hitchcock, 1951)

BIG BLUESTEM

Grass Family (Poaceae: Andropogoneae)

LATIN NAME: *Andropogon gerardii* Vitman

LONGEVITY: Perennial

SEASON: Warm

ORIGIN: Native

ECONOMIC VALUE: Wildlife - poor   Livestock - good

Considered one of the major grasses of the True (Tallgrass) Prairies, this grass is robust, growing 1-2 m (3-6.5 ft) tall. The seedhead of big bluestem is often referred to as resembling a turkey-foot because of its shape and dark color.

FLORAL CHARACTERISTICS:

Inflorescence: a panicle of 2-6 racemose branches, branches 6-10 cm (2 3/8-4 in) long, commonly 3 branched, the branches digitate or subdigitate

Spikelets: paired; sessile spikelet perfect, 0.7-1.0 cm (1/4-3/8 in) long; pedicellate spikelet sterile, nearly equal to the perfect spikelet length

Awn: glumes awnless; lemma of the sessile spikelet awned, 1-2 cm (3/8-3/4 in) long, geniculate, twisted below

Glumes: glumes indurate (hard texture), large, first glume slightly dished or grooved

VEGETATIVE CHARACTERISTICS:

Culms: 1-2 m (3-6.5 ft) tall, erect, glabrous, sparsely branched at the summit; occasionally with short rhizomes

Leaves: sheaths compressed and purplish at the base; blades flat, 10-50 cm (4-20 in) long, 0.5-1.0 cm (3/16-3/8 in) wide; collar square

Ligules: short ciliate membrane, 1.0-2.5 mm (1/32-1/10 in) long

GROWTH CHARACTERISTICS:

growth cycle is 3-4 months, numerous leaves produced in late spring, flowers late summer to early fall; reproduces by seeds, tillers, and some rhizomes

HABITAT:

prairies, dry upland sites, and open woods. Texas distribution: Areas 1-10

Andropogon ternarius
splitbeard bluestem
(inflorescence and spikelet,
Gould & Box 1965)

SPLITBEARD BLUESTEM

Grass Family (Poaceae: Andropogoneae)

LATIN NAME: *Andropogon ternarius* Michx.

LONGEVITY: Perennial

SEASON: Warm

ORIGIN: Native

ECONOMIC VALUE: Wildlife - poor   Livestock - poor

A perennial bunchgrass with short basal leaves that curl at maturity. Sheaths are slightly flattened, maroon during early growth. Seedheads of two hairy branches usually form a "V". This species is moderately shade tolerant and seldom dominates a plant community.

FLORAL CHARACTERISTICS:

Inflorescence: panicle of 2 racemose branches, paired, 3-6 cm (1 1/4-2 3/8 in) long; exserted above the uppermost part of a leaf; branches and pedicels densely villous, hairs 6-9 mm (1/4-11/32 in) long

Spikelets: paired; sessile spikelet 5-7 mm (3/16-1/4 in); lemmas hyaline; upper lemma with delicate awn, 1-2.5 cm (3/8-1 in) long; pedicellate spikelet sterile, reduced to an awnless rudiment, 2 mm (1/16 in) long

Awns: glumes awnless; upper lemma of sessile spikelet with awn 1-2.5 cm (3/8-1 in) long, geniculate

Glumes: glabrous, 5-7 mm (3/16-1/4 in) long

VEGETATIVE CHARACTERISTICS:

Culms: caespitose, 50-110 cm (19-44 in) tall, glabrous or with a long tuft of hair below upper nodes; culms with numerous axillary inflorescences

Leaves: basal and cauline; sheaths glabrous to villous to hispid; blades 20-45 cm (8-18 in) long, 2-4 mm (1/16-5/32 in) wide, flat

Ligules: ciliate membrane with minute hairs, less than 1 cm (3/8 in) long

GROWTH CHARACTERISTICS:

moderately shade tolerant, starts growth in April, flowers September to November; reproduces by seeds and tillers

HABITAT:

sandy woods and cut over pastures. Texas distribution: Areas 1-5

Andropogon virginicus
broomsedge bluestem
(Hitchcock, 1951)

BROOMSEDGE BLUESTEM

Grass Family (Poaceae: Andropogoneae)

LATIN NAME: *Andropogon virginicus* L.

LONGEVITY: Perennial

SEASON: Warm

ORIGIN: Native

ECONOMIC VALUE: Wildlife - poor   Livestock - poor

Perennial bunchgrass with both stem and basal leaves. Leaves are flat or folded, and yellowish-green with strongly flattened keels. The stem is flattened at the base. Mature plants are tawny yellow. The seedheads are numerous on any given stem, each partially enclosed by a leaf-like bract. The overall appearance of the plant resembles a broom, hence the common name. Considered an indicator of deteriorated rangeland.

FLORAL CHARACTERISTICS:

Inflorescence: panicle of 2-4 racemose branches; branches 2-3 cm (3/4-1 3/16 in) long; base included in a tawny spathe, fragile in appearance

Spikelets: paired; sessile spikelet perfect, 3-4 mm (1/8-5/32 in) long, 2 florets, fragile; pedicellate spikelet usually absent

Awns: glumes awnless, upper lemma with a delicate awn 1-2 cm (3/8-3/4 in) long

Glumes: texture indurate (hard), green to yellow green, 3-4 mm (1/8-5/32 in) long

VEGETATIVE CHARACTERISTICS:

Culms: small tufts, 0.5-1 m (1.5-3 ft) tall, flattened at base, glabrous, branched above

Leaves: sheaths compressed-keeled, overlapping, margins hairy; blades 2-5 mm (1/16-3/16 in) wide, flat or folded, orange to straw colored at maturity

Ligules: ciliate membrane, 1 mm (1/32 in) long, truncate

GROWTH CHARACTERISTICS:

starts growth when daytime temperatures average 61-63°F (16-17°C), grows in infertile soils but is not shade tolerant; reproduces by seeds and tillers

HABITAT:

open ground, old fields, sterile hills and sandy soils. Texas distribution: Areas 1-7

Bothriochloa barbinodis
cane bluestem
(Judd, 1962)

CANE BLUESTEM

Grass Family (Poaceae: Andropogoneae)

LATIN NAME: *Bothriochloa barbinodis* (Lag.) Herter var. *barbinodis*

LONGEVITY: Perennial

SEASON: Warm

ORIGIN: Native

ECONOMIC VALUE: Wildlife - poor   Livestock - fair

Often confused with silver bluestem as well as other bluestems, it is a large bunchgrass. Seedheads of cane bluestem branch from a short central axis. The branches may be nearly as long as the seedhead. This lends the fan-shaped appearance to the seedhead. The nodes of the stem are topped by a ring of hairs.

FLORAL CHARACTERISTICS:

Inflorescence: panicle 7-12 cm (2 3/4-4 3/4 in) long with several racemose branches, partially enclosed in sheath; branches and pedicels densely villous with a central groove

Spikelets: paired; sessile spikelet 4.4-7 mm (5/32-1/4 in) long; pedicellate spikelet smaller and narrower than the sessile spikelet

Awns: glumes awnless; upper lemma awn 20-30 mm (3/4-1 1/4 in) long, bent and twisted

Glumes: first glume sparsely pubescent on lower half with or without a glandular pit or pinhole

VEGETATIVE CHARACTERISTICS:

Culms: erect or geniculate at base, 50-100 cm (20-39 in) tall; nodes with a fringe of hairs, hairs 1-3 mm (1/32-1/8 in) long

Leaves: glabrous; blades 20-30 cm (8-12 in) long, 2-8 mm (1/16-5/16 in) wide, tapering

Ligules: membranous, 1-2 mm (1/32-1/16 in) long, lacerate

GROWTH CHARACTERISTICS:

starts growth when temperature is between 65°-70°F (18-21°C); inflorescence produced in midsummer, seeds mature from late summer to fall; reproduces by seeds and tillers

HABITAT:

grows well in sandy loam gravel, loam or loamy, calcareous soils. Texas distribution: Areas 2, 5-10

Bothriochloa ischaemum var. *songarica*
King Ranch bluestem
(inflorescence and spikelet,
Gould and Box, 1965)

KING RANCH BLUESTEM

Grass Family (Poaceae: Andropogoneae)

LATIN NAME:	*Bothriochloa ischaemum* (L.) Keng var. *songarica* (Rupr.) Celarier & Harlan
LONGEVITY:	Perennial
SEASON:	Warm
ORIGIN:	Introduced
ECONOMIC VALUE:	Wildlife - fair Livestock - fair

This weedy grass has been planted throughout Texas along highways to quickly stabilize soils. General appearance of the seedhead is less hairy than other bluestems. The stem is slender and commonly bent when compared to others.

FLORAL CHARACTERISTICS:

Inflorescence: panicle of 2-8 racemose branches; each branch 3-9 cm (1 1/4-3 1/2 in) long; branches and pedicels ciliate on margins, with a central groove

Spikelets: paired; one sessile, one pedicellate; sessile spikelet 3-4 mm (1/8-5/32 in) long, perfect; pedicellate spikelet sterile

Awns: glumes awnless; upper lemma awn bent, twisted, 1-1.5 mm (1/32-1/16 in) long

Glumes: first glume scabrous to hispid, apex acute, without a glandular pit

VEGETATIVE CHARACTERISTICS:

Culms: erect or decumbent or may be stoloniferous, 30-50 cm (12-20 in) tall; nodes bearded, hairs short

Leaves: sheaths glabrous; blades with papilla based hairs near base

Ligules: membranous, 1 mm (1/32 in) or less in length, truncate

GROWTH CHARACTERISTICS:

initiates growth in late spring, flowers year round under favorable moisture conditions; susceptible to leaf rust; reproduces from seeds, tillers, and occasionally stolons and rhizomes

HABITAT:

adapted best to loam and clay soils however, grows on sand in some locations. Texas distribution: Areas 2-7

Bothriochloa laguroides var. *torreyana*
silver bluestem
(Leithead, 1971)

SILVER BLUESTEM

Grass Family (Poaceae: Andropogoneae)

LATIN NAME:	*Bothriochloa laguroides* (DC.) Herter subsp. *torreyana* (Steud.) Allred & Gould (*Bothriochloa saccharoides* (Sw.) Rydb.)
LONGEVITY:	Perennial
SEASON:	Warm
ORIGIN:	Native
ECONOMIC VALUE:	Wildlife - poor Livestock - fair

A weedy perennial grass with leaves tapering to a point, has adapted to a variety of habitats. Seedheads are conspicuously hairy. Past misidentification of herbarium specimens has created confusion regarding node characteristics. Nodes of this bluestem are without conspicuous hair. Seedheads branch the entire length of the central axis, with the branches being much shorter than the length of the seedhead.

FLORAL CHARACTERISTICS:

Inflorescence: panicle of 6 or more racemose branches, 7-15 cm (2 3/4-6 in) long; terminal; branches and pedicels densely villous with a central groove

Spikelets: paired; sessile spikelet about 3 mm (1/8 in) long, perfect, florets 2; pedicellate spikelet smaller, sterile; silver white color from the hairs

Awns: glumes awnless; upper lemma awn of sessile spikelet 8-18 mm (5/16-11/16 in) long, geniculate

Glumes: indurate, first glume 2-keeled, concave; second glume 1-keeled, 3-nerved

VEGETATIVE CHARACTERISTICS:

Culms: crooked, 60-130 cm (23-51 in) tall

Leaves: sheaths glabrous, keeled near the collar; blades flat, 8-20 cm (3 1/8-8 in) long, 3-9 mm (1/8-11/32 in) wide, gradually, tapering to a point, margins white, glaucous

Ligules: membranous, 1-3 mm (1/32-1/8 in) long, erose

GROWTH CHARACTERISTICS:

starts growth in spring when daytime temperatures reach 70°F (21°C); does not grow well on moist areas; reproduces by seeds and tillers

HABITAT:

prairies and rocky slopes. Texas distribution: Areas 1-10

Heteropogon contortus
tanglehead
(Leithead, 1971)

TANGLEHEAD

Grass Family (Poaceae: Andropogoneae)

LATIN NAME: *Heteropogon contortus* (L.) Beauv.

LONGEVITY: Perennial

SEASON: Warm

ORIGIN: Native

ECONOMIC VALUE: Wildlife - poor   Livestock - good

The dark brown awns on the seeds of this grass twist and tangle together, hence the common name. Seeds at the base of the seedhead are not awned. Stems branch well above the base. Leaf margins are hairy and have scattered glands. The entire plant turns a reddish-brown color at maturity. Leaf tips are blunt.

FLORAL CHARACTERISTICS:

Inflorescence: spicate raceme, 3-10 cm (1 1/4-4 in) long, unilateral

Spikelets: paired, closely imbricate; both spikelets at base staminate or neuter, above that the sessile spikelet perfect and pedicellate spikelets staminate or neuter

Awns: glumes awnless; upper lemma awn 5-15 cm (2-6 in) long, dark brown, geniculate, tangling with other awns

Glumes: nearly equal; glumes hirsute to glabrous, brownish

VEGETATIVE CHARACTERISTICS:

Culms: erect, 20-75 cm (8-30 in) tall, flat, branched above, tufted

Leaves: basal and cauline; sheaths flat, keeled, margins glandular and hairy; blades 5-23 cm (2-9 in) long, 4-5 mm (5/32-3/16 in) wide, margins white, apex obtuse; reddish brown at maturity

Ligules: ciliate membrane, 1 mm (1/32 in) long, truncate

GROWTH CHARACTERISTICS:

starts growth in early spring, matures by August to September; reproduces by seeds and tillers

HABITAT:

rocky hills and canyons. Texas distribution: Areas 2, 6, 7, 10

Schizachyrium scoparium
little bluestem
(Hitchcock, 1951)

LITTLE BLUESTEM

Grass Family (Poaceae: Andropogoneae)

LATIN NAME: *Schizachyrium scoparium* (Michx.) Nash var. *scoparium*

LONGEVITY: Perennial

SEASON: Cool

ORIGIN: Native

ECONOMIC VALUE: Wildlife - poor   Livestock - good

Another important grass of the True Prairie, this grass is blue-green turning to a reddish-brown at maturity. Erect stems arise from a densely leafy base. Seeds are not as hairy as silver, cane, splitbeard, or broomsedge bluestems and not as robust as big bluestem. Seeds grow one on top of each other and break apart at the jointed end of each seed at maturity. Excellent nesting cover for birds.

FLORAL CHARACTERISTICS:

Inflorescence: spicate raceme, 2.5-5 cm (1-2 in) long; numerous inflorescences per culm; rachis and pedicels pilose

Spikelets: paired; sessile spikelet perfect, 6-8 mm (1/4-5/16 in) long; pedicellate spikelet sterile, usually much shorter than sessile spikelet

Awns: glumes awnless; upper lemma of sessile spikelet awned, about 1-2 cm (3/8-3/4 in) long, geniculate and twisted

Glumes: thickened, indurate, concave

VEGETATIVE CHARACTERISTICS:

Culms: base decumbent otherwise erect, 0.5-2 m (20-80 in) tall, caespitose, base leafy

Leaves: basal and cauline; sheaths keeled, glabrous; blades 8-25 cm (3 1/8-10 in) long, 2-6 mm (1/16-1/4 in) wide, glabrous to scabrous

Ligules: ciliate membrane, 1-3 mm (1/32-1/8 in) long, truncate to rounded

GROWTH CHARACTERISTICS:

growth starts in late spring, matures in early fall; seeds mature in October to November; reproduces by seeds and tillers

HABITAT:

grows on a variety of soils; prairies, savannahs. Texas distribution: Areas 2-10

Sorghum halepense
johnsongrass
(Hitchcock, 1951)

JOHNSONGRASS

Grass Family (Poaceae: Andropogoneae)

LATIN NAME: *Sorghum halepense* (L.) Pers.

LONGEVITY: Perennial

SEASON: Warm

ORIGIN: Introduced

ECONOMIC VALUE: Wildlife - fair   Livestock - good (poisonous)

This weedy grass occurs throughout Texas. It is a tall grass with scaly rhizomes. Leaves are wide with a strong, lightly colored midvein and splotches of purple caused by fungi. The seedhead is large and open, usually with 4 or more branches coming off from a common point on the main axis.

FLORAL CHARACTERISTICS:

Inflorescence: large open panicle, 15-40 cm (6-16 in) long; spikelets in pairs, one sessile and perfect, the other pedicellate and staminate

Spikelets: sessile spikelets frequently turning purple, 4-6 mm (5/32-1/4 in) long, shiny at apex; pedicellate spikelets narrower, and thinner with conspicuous nerves

Awns: glumes awnless; upper lemmas awnless or awned; awn 1-1.5 cm (3/8-9/16 in) long, geniculate

Glumes: indurate, nerveless, 2-6 mm (1/16-1/4 in) long

VEGETATIVE CHARACTERISTICS:

Culms: erect from coarse rhizomes, 1-2 m (3-6 ft) tall

Leaves: blades glabrous, 9-20 mm (11/32-3/4 in) wide with a broad white midrib

Ligules: ciliate membrane, 3-6 mm (1/8-1/4 in) long, truncate

GROWTH CHARACTERISTICS:

initiates growth in mid-spring, flowers year-long, spring inflorescences usually stunted with smut; fair drought tolerance and cold tolerance; stress conditions cause production of prussic acid; reproduces by seeds, tillers, and rhizomes

HABITAT:

adapted to fertile sites on a variety of soils. Texas distribution: Areas 1-10

Sorghastrum nutans
yellow indiangrass
(Gould and Box, 1965)

YELLOW INDIANGRASS

Grass Family (Poaceae: Andropogoneae)

LATIN NAME: *Sorghastrum nutans* (L.) Nash

LONGEVITY: Perennial

SEASON: Warm

ORIGIN: Native

ECONOMIC VALUE: Wildlife - fair   Livestock - good

One of the four primary grasses of the True Prairie, this tall, robust grass has short, scaly rhizomes. Stem nodes have long, soft hairs. The large "rabbit-ear" auricle is often easily visible, even on plant mounts. Seeds on the yellow-gold seedhead have bent, twisted awns.

FLORAL CHARACTERISTICS:

Inflorescence: panicle, 15-30 cm (6-12 in) long, 2-6 cm (3/4-2 3/8 in) wide, dense, yellow to tawny gold

Spikelets: paired; sessile spikelet 6-8 mm (1/4-5/16 in) long, perfect; pedicellate spikelet absent, pedicel present

Awns: glumes awnless; upper lemma of sessile spikelet with an awn 1-2 cm (3/8-3/4 in) long, once-geniculate

Glumes: indurate, brown or yellow, the first glume clasping the second

VEGETATIVE CHARACTERISTICS:

Culms: erect, 1-2 m (3-6 ft) tall, nodes pubescent; short scaly rhizomes

Leaves: sheaths rounded, pilose near the collar; auricles leaf-like, erect; blades flat or keeled, 10-30 cm (4-12 in) long, 5-10 mm (3/16-3/8 in) wide

Ligules: membranous, 2-5 mm (1/16-3/16 in) long; between the erect leaf-like auricles

GROWTH CHARACTERISTICS:

starts growth in mid-spring from short rhizomes; a good seed producer, seeds mature September to November

HABITAT:

adapted to fertile, moist soils from heavy clays to sands; prairies, savannahs, and meadows. Texas distribution: Areas 1-10

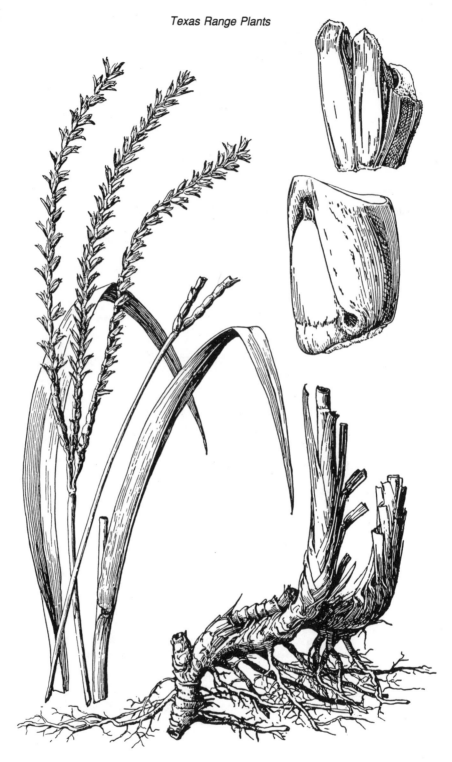

Tripsacum dactyloides
eastern gamagrass
(Hitchcock, 1951)

EASTERN GAMAGRASS

Grass Family (Poaceae: Andropogoneae)

LATIN NAME:	*Tripsacum dactyloides* (L.) L.
LONGEVITY:	Perennial
SEASON:	Warm
ORIGIN:	Native
ECONOMIC VALUE:	Wildlife - fair Livestock - good

This grass is very large and robust, arising from thick, scaly rhizomes. The wide leaves have rough, sharp edges. The seedhead is one to three long spikes with female seeds resembling hard beads at the bottom and pairs of male seeds stacked above (like the tassels of corn).

FLORAL CHARACTERISTICS:

Inflorescence: panicle of 1-3 racemose branches; branches 10-30 cm (4-12 in) long; pistillate spikelets at branch base; staminate spikelets above

Spikelets: unisexual; pistillate spikelet embedded in branch, hard, bead-like, 7-10 mm (5/16-3/8 in) long; staminate spikelet leaf-like in texture

Awns: glumes and lemmas awnless

Glumes: pistillate spikelet glumes indurate; staminate spikelet glumes leaf-like in texture

VEGETATIVE CHARACTERISTICS:

Culms: tufted, 1-3 m (3-10 ft.) tall, erect to ascending; forming large colonies from thick rhizomes

Leaves: basal and cauline; sheaths glabrous, rounded; blades flat, 30-70 cm (12-28 in) long, 10-40 mm (3/8-1 1/4 in) wide, scabrous above and on the margins

Ligules: ciliate membrane, 1-2 mm (1/32-1/16 in) long, truncate

GROWTH CHARACTERISTICS:

poor seed producer, reproduces by rhizomes; most growth in spring, but plants remain green until frost in the fall of the year

HABITAT:

grows well on moist, well-drained soils; moist sites, swales, meadows, and stream banks. Texas distribution: Areas 1-5, 7-10

Aristida oligantha
oldfield threeawn
(Gould and Box, 1965)

OLDFIELD THREEAWN

Grass Family (Poaceae: Aristideae)

LATIN NAME: *Aristida oligantha* Michx.

LONGEVITY: Annual

SEASON: Warm

ORIGIN: Native

ECONOMIC VALUE: Wildlife - poor   Livestock - poor

This annual shortgrass is named for its habit of establishing in abandoned cropland, fields and other disturbed sites. The seeds have three awns of equal length. The plant characteristically branches at the stem nodes.

FLORAL CHARACTERISTICS:

Inflorescence: panicle, 10-20 cm (4-8 in) long, open

Spikelets: floret 1; short pedicellate

Awns: glumes awnless; lemma awn column branches into 3 awns, awns 4-7 cm (1 1/2-2 3/4 in) long, tapering to an awn-like point

Glumes: more or less equal, 2-3 cm (3/4-1 1/4 in) long, tapering to an awn-like point

VEGETATIVE CHARACTERISTICS:

Culms: ascending, 15-50 cm (6-20 in) tall, frequently branching at lower culm nodes

Leaves: sheaths rounded, mostly glabrous; blades few, 10-20 cm (4-8 in) long, 2-4 mm (1/16-5/32 in) wide, usually flat

Ligules: ciliate membrane, 0.5 mm (1/64 in) long

GROWTH CHARACTERISTICS:

starts growth in early spring; completes life cycle in 2 months; reproduces by seeds

HABITAT:

weed, disturbed areas of open, dry ground. Texas distribution: Areas 1-10

Aristida purpurea
threeawn
(Hitchcock, 1951)

THREEAWN (Perennial threeawn)

Grass Family (Poaceae: Aristideae)

LATIN NAME: *Aristida purpurea* Nutt.

LONGEVITY: Perennial

SEASON: Warm

ORIGIN: Native

ECONOMIC VALUE: Wildlife - poor   Livestock - fair / poor

This perennial threeawn is a densely tufted plant which livestock will utilize somewhat before seedheads form. Unlike oldfield threeawn, the stems of this threeawn do not branch. Long hair at the margins of the collar also characterizes perennial threeawn.

FLORAL CHARACTERISTICS:

Inflorescence: panicle, 10-30 cm (4-12 in) long, contracted, occasionally lower branches slightly spreading

Spikelets: floret 1; lemma 3-nerved, scabrous, with a slightly twisted awn column

Awns: glumes awnless; lemma column branches into 3 awns, awns nearly equal, 15-40 mm (9/16-1 1/2 in) long

Glumes: unequal, broad; second glume longer, 11-15 mm long

VEGETATIVE CHARACTERISTICS:

Culms: tufted, 35-80 cm (14-31 in) tall, erect to ascending

Leaves: glaucous; sheaths glabrous, collar with long hairs on margins; blades involute, 10-25 cm (4-10 in) long, 1-2 mm (1/32-1/16 in) wide, scabrous

Ligules: ciliate membrane, 0.5 mm (1/64 in) or less long

GROWTH CHARACTERISTICS:

flowers May to October, reproduces by seeds and tillers

HABITAT:

dry plains, gravelly or sandy soils. Texas distribution: Areas 4-10

Bouteloua curtipendula
sideoats grama
(Judd, 1962)

SIDEOATS GRAMA

Grass Family (Poaceae: Chlorideae)

LATIN NAME: *Bouteloua curtipendula* (Michx.) Torr.

LONGEVITY: Perennial

SEASON: Warm

ORIGIN: Native

ECONOMIC VALUE: Wildlife - good   Livestock - good

The State Grass of Texas, the common name of sideoats grama refers to the arrangement of the seeds hanging off of one side of the panicle. The glandular-based hairs on the leaf margins also distinguish this plant. This midgrass grows throughout the State and was designated State Grass in 1971.

FLORAL CHARACTERISTICS:

Inflorescence: panicle of 35-80 spicate primary unilateral branches; panicle 10-30 cm (4-12 in) long, branches 1-2 cm (3/8-3/4 in) long; individual branches turned to one side of inflorescence

Spikelets: florets 2, lower perfect, upper reduced to 3 awns; lemmas 3-nerved; spikelets pendulous

Awns: glumes awnless; lemma awnless or with a short awn 1-2 mm (1/32-1/16 in) long

Glumes: unequal, tapering 0.6-1 cm (1/4-3/8 in) long

VEGETATIVE CHARACTERISTICS:

Culms: erect, 20-100 cm (8-39 in) tall, caespitose or rhizomatous

Leaves: mostly basal; sheaths round, glabrous; collar pilose on margins; blades flat to involute, 2-30 cm (3/4-12 in) long, 2-4 mm (1/16-1/8 in) wide, papillose hairs on the margins

Ligules: ciliate membrane, 0.5 mm (less than 1/32 in) long

GROWTH CHARACTERISTICS:

starts growth in early spring; flowers July to September; reproduces by seeds and tillers, and one variety has rhizomes

HABITAT:

well adapted to calcareous and moderately alkaline soils; rocky shallow sites of prairies. Texas distribution: Areas 2-10

Bouteloua eriopoda
black grama
(Gould, 1951)

BLACK GRAMA

Grass Family (Poaceae: Chlorideae)

LATIN NAME: *Bouteloua eriopoda* (Torr.) Torr.

LONGEVITY: Perennial

SEASON: Warm

ORIGIN: Native

ECONOMIC VALUE: Wildlife - good   Livestock - good

This grass has minimal tolerance to grazing, therefore it is often located in protected areas or sites where grazing is less likely to occur. The fuzzy stems and smooth leaf sheaths give the appearance of alternating fuzzy and smooth segments the length of the stem. The seedhead is delicate or fragile in appearance.

FLORAL CHARACTERISTICS:

Inflorescence: panicle of 3-8 spicate primary unilateral branches; branches 2-5 cm (3/4-2 in) long, straight to curved, delicate, with 12-20 spikelets, comb-like

Spikelets: florets 2; lemmas 7-10 mm (1/4-3/8 in) long, 3-nerved

Awns: glumes awnless; lower lemma awn 1.5-3 mm (1/32-1/8 in) long; upper lemma 3-awned, awns 4-8 mm (5/32-5/16 in) long

Glumes: unequal, lanceolate, pointed; first glume less than one-half the length of the second

VEGETATIVE CHARACTERISTICS:

Culms: decumbent to erect, stoloniferous, slender; internodes arched or bent, lanate to woolly pubescent; base swollen, woolly

Leaves: mostly basal; sheaths glabrous; blades 0.5-2 mm (less than 1/32-1/16 in) wide, arched, hairy above

Ligules: ring of hairs

GROWTH CHARACTERISTICS:

starts growth in July, low seed viability; reproduces primarily by stolons; frequently occurs in nearly pure stands; frequently killed by overgrazing

HABITAT:

plateaus, hills, and desert grasslands. Texas distribution: Areas 7-10

Bouteloua gracilis
blue grama
(Hitchcock, 1951)

BLUE GRAMA

Grass Family (Poaceae: Chlorideae)

LATIN NAME:	*Bouteloua gracilis* (H.B.K.) Lag. *ex* Griffiths
LONGEVITY:	Perennial
SEASON:	Warm
ORIGIN:	Native
ECONOMIC VALUE:	Wildlife - good Livestock - good

More tolerant of grazing than black grama, blue grama is adapted to a variety of sites. The seedhead is composed of 1-3 comb-like branches. This short grass is one of the major dominants of the Great Plains. The plant base is curved rather than straight.

FLORAL CHARACTERISTICS:

Inflorescence: a panicle of 1-3 spicate primary unilateral or comb-like branches, branches with 40-90 spikelets, branch 1.5-5 cm (1/32-3/16 in) long

Spikelets: 4-5 mm (5/32-3/16 in) long, 1 perfect floret and at least 1 reduced floret; lemma pubescent at base, 3-nerved

Awns: glumes awnless; lemma awns usually 3, 1-3 mm (1/32-1/8 in) long

Glumes: unequal, 1-nerved, glabrous or with papilla-based hairs on the midnerve

VEGETATIVE CHARACTERISTICS:

Culms: erect, 20-70 cm (8-28 in) tall, usually a bunchgrass

Leaves: mainly basal; sheaths glabrous to pilose; blades 5-10 cm (2-4 in) long, 2-5 mm (1/16-3/16 in) wide, flat

Ligules: ring of soft hairs, 0.5 mm (less than 1/32 in) long

GROWTH CHARACTERISTICS:

growth begins in early summer, matures in about 2 months; growth frequently controlled by available moisture; reproduces by seeds and tillers

HABITAT:

grows well on sandy loam and loam, but occurs on sand, clay, or gravel; some salt tolerance. Texas distribution: Areas 5, 7-10

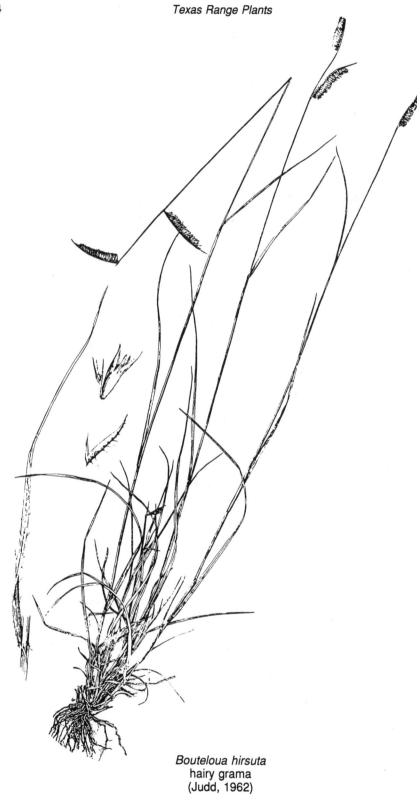

Bouteloua hirsuta
hairy grama
(Judd, 1962)

HAIRY GRAMA

Grass Family (Poaceae: Chlorideae)

LATIN NAME: *Bouteloua hirsuta* Lag.

LONGEVITY: Perennial

SEASON: Warm

ORIGIN: Native

ECONOMIC VALUE: Wildlife - fair   Livestock - fair

This erect growing short grass has more branches in the seedhead than blue grama. These branches are characterized by a "stinger" or tip at the end of each branch. Close examination of the seedhead reveals dark glandular based hairs which also can be found at the base of leaf blade margins.

FLORAL CHARACTERISTICS:

Inflorescence: a panicle of 1-4 spicate primary unilateral (comb-like) branches that are 2.5-3.5 cm (1/16-5/32 in) long, dark papilla-based hairs on branches, primary branch extends beyond the point of spikelet attachment

Spikelets: 20-50 per branch; about 6 mm (1/4 in) long with 1 perfect floret and 1-3 reduced florets

Awns: glumes awnless; upper floret lemma with 3 awns, awns about 4 mm (5/32 in) long

Glumes: unequal, the first short; second glume 3-5 mm (1/8-3/16 in) long, tuberculate hispid

VEGETATIVE CHARACTERISTICS:

Culms: tufted, 15-55 cm (6-22 in) long with 4-8 nodes

Leaves: sheaths glabrous; collar hairy with glandular margins; blades flat or involute, 3-10 cm (1 1/4-4 in) long, 1-3 mm (1/32-1/8 in) wide, base with glandular margins

Ligules: membranous, 0.25 mm (less than 1/32 in) long, truncate

GROWTH CHARACTERISTICS:

starts growth by mid-July or when moisture is available; reproduces by seeds and tillers

HABITAT:

dry, rough, rocky ridges; loose sands or shallow upland sites. Texas distribution: Areas 1-10

Bouteloua rigidiseta
Texas grama
(inflorescence, Gould and Box, 1965)
(spikelet, Hitchcock, 1951)

TEXAS GRAMA

Grass Family (Poaceae: Chlorideae)

LATIN NAME: *Bouteloua rigidiseta* (Steud.) Hitchc.

LONGEVITY: Perennial

SEASON: Warm

ORIGIN: Native

ECONOMIC VALUE: Wildlife - poor   Livestock - poor

Texas grama is a small grass with short leaves which taper to a sharp point. The seeds are borne in bell-shaped clusters along the seedhead. These bristly clusters usually appear more open than those of sideoats grama.

FLORAL CHARACTERISTICS:

Inflorescence: panicle, 3-15 cm (1 1/4-6 in) long; spicate primary unilateral branches with 3-5 spikelets, short, alternate, the spikelet cluster wedge shaped; primary branches 0.8-1.6 mm (less than 1/32-1/16 in) long

Spikelets: 2 florets, uppermost greatly reduced; lowermost lemma 2-4 mm (1/16-5/32 in) long, 3-nerved, the nerves extending into awns

Awns: second glume with a short stout awn extending from between the lobes of a lobed apex; lemmas with 3 awns, upper lemma awns 3-10 mm (1/8-3/8 in) long

Glumes: glumes unequal, first shorter than second

VEGETATIVE CHARACTERISTICS:

Culms: tufted, 12-45 cm (4 3/4-18 in) tall, erect to ascending

Leaves: blades flat, 5-16 cm (2-6 1/4 in) long, 1-2 mm (1/32-1/16) wide, pilose

Ligules: ciliate membrane, 0.1-0.3 mm (less than 1/64 in) long, minute

GROWTH CHARACTERISTICS:

flowers from April to November when adequate moisture is available; reproduces by seeds and tillers

HABITAT:

prairies, savannahs and right-of-ways; frequently in disturbed sites. Texas distribution: Areas 2-10

Bouteloua trifida
red grama
(Gould and Box, 1965)

RED GRAMA

Grass Family (Poaceae: Chlorideae)

LATIN NAME: *Bouteloua trifida* Thurb. in Wats.

LONGEVITY: Perennial

SEASON: Warm

ORIGIN: Native

ECONOMIC VALUE: Wildlife - poor   Livestock - poor

This shortgrass has fewer seeds than blue or hairy grama, thus the combs appear less tightly packed. The seedhead is also bristly. The leaf blades are the shortest and narrowest of all the gramas considered here.

FLORAL CHARACTERISTICS:

Inflorescence: panicle of 2-7 spicate primary unilateral branches; branches alternate, 1.2-2.5 cm (1/2-1 in) long with less than 35 spikelets

Spikelets: 2 florets; lower floret perfect, about 2 mm (1/16 in) long; upper floret rudimentary

Awns: glumes awnless; lower lemma awn about 4 mm (5/32 in) long; upper lemma awn 3.5 mm (1/8-1/4 in) long, rudiment with 3 awns

Glumes: unequal, glabrous, acute to acuminate

VEGETATIVE CHARACTERISTICS:

Culms: ascending to erect, 10-40 cm (4-16 in) tall; base firm and slightly rhizomatous

Leaves: mostly basal, glabrous; blades 4-8 cm (1 1/2-3 1/8 in) long, about 1.5 mm (1/32 in) wide, flat or folded

Ligules: ciliate membrane, 0.1-0.3 mm (less than 1/64 in) long, minute

GROWTH CHARACTERISTICS:

flowers whenever moisture and temperature are adequate, persists under heavy grazing; reproduces by seeds, tillers, and occasional rhizomes

HABITAT:

adapted to shallow, gravelly soil with poor moisture conditions; dry rocky sites. Texas distribution: Areas 2, 3, 5-10

Buchloe dactyloides
buffalograss
(Judd, 1962)

BUFFALOGRASS

Grass Family (Poaceae: Chlorideae)

LATIN NAME: *Buchloe dactyloides* (Nutt.) Engelm.

LONGEVITY: Perennial

SEASON: Warm

ORIGIN: Native

ECONOMIC VALUE: Wildlife - fair   Livestock - good

This shortgrass has both rhizomes and stolons. Leaves are sparsely hairy while the stem and stolon nodes are without hair. Male and female plants grow separately. Female plants bear seed in bur-like clusters among the leaves. Males have 2-3 flag-like seedheads borne above the leaves. This species is highly drought resistant and a former dominant of the Great Plains grasslands.

FLORAL CHARACTERISTICS:

Inflorescence: staminate plants have panicles of 1-2 spicate primary unilateral branches; pistillate plants have bur-like clusters of spikelets

Spikelets: staminate spikelets with 2 florets, florets 4.5-5 mm (5/32-1/4 in) long; pistillate spikelets with 1 floret in bur-like clusters of 3-7

Awns: glumes, lemmas, and paleas awnless

Glumes: unequal in both pistillate and staminate spikelets

VEGETATIVE CHARACTERISTICS:

Culms: nodes glabrous; culm of staminate plants erect, 5-25 cm (2-10 in) tall; culm of pistillate plants included within the leaves; with extensive stolons

Leaves: sheaths rounded, mostly glabrous; blades curly, 2-15 cm (3/4-6 in) long, 1-2.5 mm (1/32-1/8 in) wide, flat, sparsely pilose

Ligules: a ciliate membrane, 0.5-1 mm (1/32 in or less) long

GROWTH CHARACTERISTICS:

plants dioecious; starts growth when temperatures reach 68°F (20°C), grows while adequate moisture is available; seed matures in 6 weeks; reproduces by seeds, tillers, and stolons

HABITAT:

dry prairies on medium to fine textured soils; occasionally used as a lawn grass. Texas distribution: Areas 1-10

Chloris cucullata
hooded windmillgrass
(inflorescence and spikelet,
Gould and Box, 1965)

HOODED WINDMILLGRASS

Grass Family (Poaceae: Chlorideae)

LATIN NAME: *Chloris cucullata* Bisch.

LONGEVITY: Perennial

SEASON: Warm

ORIGIN: Native

ECONOMIC VALUE: Wildlife - fair   Livestock - fair

This plant is a shortgrass with a windmill-shaped seedhead, hence both windmillgrasses, hooded and tumble, are named for the seedhead appearance. Seeds of hooded windmillgrass appear inflated. Awns are shorter than those of tumble windmillgrass. Leaves are basal and both leaves and sheaths are flattened.

FLORAL CHARACTERISTICS:

Inflorescence: panicle of digitate or subdigitate spicate primary unilateral branches; branches 2-5 cm (3/4-2 in) long, curved, numerous

Spikelets: appear inflated, crowded, with 2 florets; lemmas 3-nerved, brownish at maturity

Awns: glumes awnless; lemma awn to 1.5 mm (1/16 in) long

Glumes: unequal, lanceolate; first glume 0.5-0.7 mm (less than 1/32 in) long; second glume 1-1.5 mm (1/32-1/16 in) long

VEGETATIVE CHARACTERISTICS:

Culms: erect, 15-50 cm (6-20 in) tall, tufted, base flattened

Leaves: basal and cauline; sheaths keeled, glabrous with white margins; blades 5-20 cm (2-8 in) long, 2-5 mm (1/16-3/16 in) wide, folded, apex blunt, glabrous to scabrous

Ligules: ciliate membrane, 1-2 mm (1/32-1/16 in) long, rounded

GROWTH CHARACTERISTICS:

starts growth in April; may flower several times per year; reproduces by seeds and tillers

HABITAT:

plains, prairies, savannahs, particularly on sandy soils. Texas distribution: Areas 2, 4-10

Chloris verticillata
tumble windmillgrass
(Gould and Box, 1965)

TUMBLE WINDMILLGRASS

Grass Family (Poaceae: Chlorideae)

LATIN NAME: *Chloris verticillata* Nutt.

LONGEVITY: Perennial

SEASON: Warm

ORIGIN: Native

ECONOMIC VALUE: Wildlife - poor   Livestock - poor

A shortgrass with a seedhead of two or more sets of windmill-like branches. Seeds of this plant do not appear inflated and have longer awns than hooded windmillgrass. Leaves are primarily basal with both the blades and sheaths flattened.

FLORAL CHARACTERISTICS:

Inflorescence: panicle of 10-16 spicate primary unilateral branches; branches 7-18 cm (2 3/4-7 in) long in 2-4 verticils

Spikelets: appressed, 2-3.6 mm (1/16-5/32 in) long, 2 florets, yellowish, widely spaced on branches; lemmas elliptic to lanceolate, keel glabrous, apex acute to obtuse

Awns: glumes awnless; lemma awn 4-9 mm (5/32-11/32 in) long

Glumes: lanceolate, glabrous; first glume 2-3 mm (1/16-1/8 in) long; second glume 2.5-3.5 mm (3/32-5/32 in) long

VEGETATIVE CHARACTERISTICS:

Culms: erect to decumbent, 15-45 cm (6-18 in) tall, glabrous, occasionally branching at lower nodes

Leaves: basal and cauline; sheaths glabrous with white margins; blades 5-15 cm (2-6 in) long, 2-4 mm (1/16-5/32 in) wide, glabrous to scabrous

Ligules: ciliate membrane, 0.5-2 mm (less than 1/32-1/16 in) long

GROWTH CHARACTERISTICS:

flowers May to September; reproduces by seeds and tillers

HABITAT:

heavy clay, to sands or gravelly soils on disturbed sites. Texas distribution: Areas 1-10

Cynodon dactylon
bermudagrass
(Hitchcock, 1951)

BERMUDAGRASS

Grass Family (Poaceae: Chlorideae)

LATIN NAME: *Cynodon dactylon* (L.) Pers.

LONGEVITY: Perennial

SEASON: Warm

ORIGIN: Introduced

ECONOMIC VALUE: Wildlife - poor   Livestock - good

A low growing grass with rhizomes and stolons. The seedhead has 2-5 branches appearing like a delicate windmill. These branches are divergent at maturity while those of common carpetgrass remain ascending. The seeds lay in two rows on each branch, do not appear inflated, and lack an awn. Leaves can appear conspicuously 2-ranked.

FLORAL CHARACTERISTICS:

Inflorescence: panicle of 2-5 digitate spicate primary unilateral branches; branches 2-6 cm (3/4-2 3/8 in) long

Spikelets: sessile, 2-2.5 mm (1/16-3/32 in) long, in 2 rows on the lower side of the branch; not appearing inflated; 1 floret; lemma 3-nerved

Awns: glumes, lemmas, and paleas awnless

Glumes: subequal, lanceolate, 1-nerved, 1.5-2 mm (1/32-1/16 in) long

VEGETATIVE CHARACTERISTICS:

Culms: flattened, 10-50 cm (4-20 in) tall, weak, mat-forming; scaly rhizomes and/or stolons

Leaves: sheaths round, glabrous except for a tuft of hair on the sides of the collar; blades flat, 3-12 cm (1 1/4-4 3/4 in) long, 1-3 mm (1/32-1/8 in) wide, occasionally folded, pilose on the upper surface

Ligules: membranous, 0.2-0.5 mm (less than 1/32 in) long

GROWTH CHARACTERISTICS:

high salt tolerance; reproduces by seeds, tillers, rhizomes, and stolons

HABITAT:

waste places, weedy habitats, fields; planted in pastures and lawns; Texas distribution: Areas 1-10

Hilaria belangeri
curly mesquite
(Judd, 1962)

CURLY MESQUITE

Grass Family (Poaceae: Chlorideae)

LATIN NAME: *Hilaria belangeri* (Steud.) Nash

LONGEVITY: Perennial

SEASON: Warm

ORIGIN: Native

ECONOMIC VALUE: Wildlife - poor   Livestock - fair

Most often confused with buffalograss, this grass also has both rhizomes and stolons. It does not, however, bear male and female flowers on separate plants as does buffalograss. The seedhead has the main axis of the seedhead strongly bent at each node. The nodes of the stems and stolons of the plants are softly fuzzy.

FLORAL CHARACTERISTICS:

Inflorescence: a spike, 2-3.5 cm (1/16-5/32 in) long; 3 spikelets per node with 4-8 nodes per inflorescence; rachis strongly angled at the nodes

Spikelets: sessile, 4.5-6 mm (5/32-1/4 in) long; lateral spikelets staminate, central spikelet perfect

Awns: midnerve of glumes extend into a short awn; lemmas awnless

Glumes: glumes of lateral spikelets scabrous, united below, broadened above; glumes of central spikelet nearly equal

VEGETATIVE CHARACTERISTICS:

Culms: erect, 10-30 cm (4-12 in) tall, nodes villous; slender stolons with wiry internodes

Leaves: sheaths glabrous; blades flat or involute, 5-20 cm (2-8 in) long, 1-2 mm (1/32-1/16 in) wide, scabrous to pilose

Ligules: membranous, 0.5-1.5 mm (less than 1/32-1/16 in) long, erose

GROWTH CHARACTERISTICS:

starts growth in late spring; highly drought resistant; productive forage species considering plant size; reproduces by seeds, tillers, and stolons

HABITAT:

adapted to many sites; deep to rocky soils; slopes and dry hillsides. Texas distribution: Areas 2, 4-10

Hilaria mutica
tobosa
(Judd, 1962)

TOBOSA

Grass Family (Poaceae: Chlorideae)

LATIN NAME: *Hilaria mutica* (Buckl.) Benth.

LONGEVITY: Perennial

SEASON: Warm

ORIGIN: Native

ECONOMIC VALUE: Wildlife - poor   Livestock - fair

This strongly rhizomatous grass is often burned to increase its palability to livestock. The central stem of the seedhead is wavy and remains after the seeds have dropped. The seeds appear papery and fan-shaped with torn edges.

FLORAL CHARACTERISTICS:

Inflorescence: spike, 4-6 cm (5/32-1/4 in) long, rachis wavy, 3 spikelets per node

Spikelets: sessile, 6-9 mm (1/4-11/32 in) long, clusters fan-shaped; central spikelet perfect; lateral spikelets staminate; lemmas 3-nerved

Awns: glumes of lateral spikelets with hairy awn to 3 mm (1/8 in) long; glumes of central spikelet mucronate; lemmas awnless

Glumes: glumes of lateral spikelets fan-shaped, apex erose

VEGETATIVE CHARACTERISTICS:

Culms: base decumbent, 30-60 cm (12-24 in) tall, wiry, lower nodes pubescent, upper nodes glabrous; rhizomes

Leaves: basal and cauline; sheaths glabrous, collar hairy near the margins; blades flat to inrolled, 5-10 cm (2-4 in) long, 2-4 mm (1/16-5/32 in) wide, glabrous

Ligules: ciliate membrane, 1-2 mm (1/32-1/16 in) long, truncate

GROWTH CHARACTERISTICS:

low seed production, reproduces primarily from rhizomes; starts growth when adequate temperature and moisture are available

HABITAT:

dry plains, heavy soils of playas, dry slopes. Texas distribution: Areas 6-10

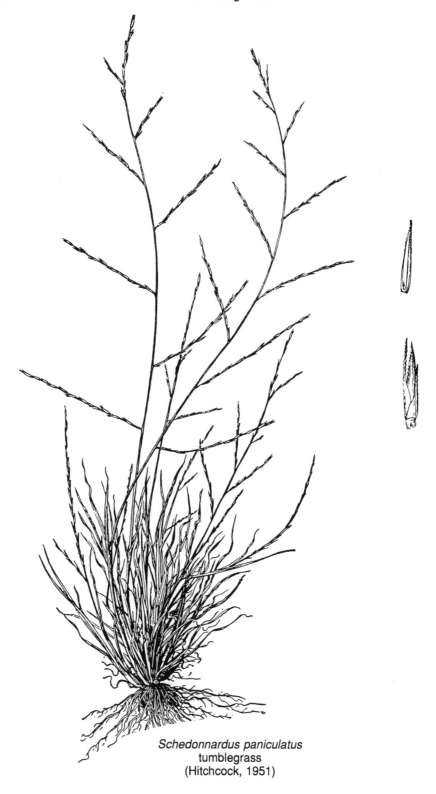

Schedonnardus paniculatus
tumblegrass
(Hitchcock, 1951)

TUMBLEGRASS

Grass Family (Poaceae: Chlorideae)

LATIN NAME: *Schedonnardus paniculatus* (Nutt.) Trel.

LONGEVITY: Perennial

SEASON: Warm

ORIGIN: Native

ECONOMIC VALUE: Wildlife - poor   Livestock - poor

This low growing grass is quickly recognized by its many spirally twisted basal leaves with white margins. The stems are slender and curved, with seeds borne very tightly in two rows to the branches of the seedhead. The entire seedhead breaks off at maturity and tumbles in the wind, hence the common name.

FLORAL CHARACTERISTICS:

Inflorescence: panicle, 30-60 cm (12-24 in) long, 5-30 cm (2-12 in) wide, of several spicate primary unilateral branches, disarticulates at the base at maturity; branches alternate, few, curved at maturity

Spikelets: 1 floret, 3-4 mm (1/8-5/32 in) long, slender; imbedded in the branches

Awns: glumes, lemma, and palea awnless

Glumes: unequal, 1-nerved; the second as long as the lemma

VEGETATIVE CHARACTERISTICS:

Culms: erect to decumbent, 10-70 cm (4-28 in) long, stiffly curving

Leaves: mainly basal; sheaths keeled; blades 2-15 cm (3/4-6 in) long, 1-2 mm (1/32-1/16 in) wide, twisted, margins white and scabrous

Ligules: membranous, 2-3 mm (1/16-1/8 in) long, rounded to obtuse

GROWTH CHARACTERISTICS:

grows throughout the spring, summer, or fall when there is available moisture; reproduces by seeds and tillers

HABITAT:

disturbed sites; lower successional stages. Texas distribution: Areas 1-10

Spartina patens
marshhay cordgrass
(Leithead, 1971)

MARSHHAY CORDGRASS

Grass Family (Poaceae: Chlorideae)

LATIN NAME:	*Spartina patens* (Ait.) Muhl.
LONGEVITY:	Perennial
SEASON:	Warm
ORIGIN:	Native
ECONOMIC VALUE:	Wildlife - poor Livestock - good

This cordgrass has slender stems arising from rhizomes. There are 2-4 branches bearing the seeds. These branches are fewer and longer than those of gulf cordgrass. The branches spread away from the main axis rather than being tightly ascending as in gulf cordgrass. The seeds are borne on one side of the comb-like branches.

FLORAL CHARACTERISTICS:

Inflorescence: panicle of 2-7 spicate primary unilateral branches; branches alternate, 3-9 cm (1 1/4-3 /12 in) long; spikelets appressed to branches

Spikelets: 1 floret; lemma 7-12 mm (1/4-1/2 in) long, 3-nerved; palea slightly longer than lemma

Awns: glumes and lemma awnless

Glumes: unequal, first glume one-half spikelet length or less; second glume scabrous on the nerve, equal spikelet length

VEGETATIVE CHARACTERISTICS:

Culms: erect to ascending, single or small tufts, 0.5-1.3 m (20-50 in) tall; rhizomatous

Leaves: basal and cauline; sheaths rounded, glabrous; blades narrow, usually involute, 1-5 mm (1/32-3/16 in) wide

Ligules: a ring of hairs, minute

GROWTH CHARACTERISTICS:

growth starts in April; reproduces by seeds, tillers, and rhizomes

HABITAT:

margins of salt marshes and sandy meadows of the coast. Texas distribution: Area 2

Spartina spartinae
gulf cordgrass
(base and leaves, Leithead, 1971)
(inflorescence and spikelet, Gould and Box, 1965)

GULF CORDGRASS

Grass Family (Poaceae: Chlorideae)

LATIN NAME: *Spartina spartinae* (Trin.) Merr.

LONGEVITY: Perennial

SEASON: Warm

ORIGIN: Native

ECONOMIC VALUE: Wildlife - poor   Livestock - fair

Leaves of this stout, coarse grass roll inward at maturity, resembling a cord. The seedhead is short and very compressed with the branches laying very close to the main axis. Branches bearing the seeds are more numerous and shorter than those of marshhay cordgrass. The rough seeds are borne on three sides of the branches.

FLORAL CHARACTERISTICS:

Inflorescence: panicle, 13-23 cm (1/2-1 in) long, of 15-30 spicate primary unilateral branches; branches mostly alternate, 2-4 cm (3/4-1 1/2 in) long and crowded on the central axis, tightly ascending

Spikelets: scabrous, 6-8 mm (1/4-5/16 in) long, appressed to branches, 1 floret; lemma blunt, scabrous, 3-nerved

Awns: glumes awnless to short awned; lemmas awnless to short awned; paleas awnless

Glumes: first glume one-half as long as the second, second glume blunt

VEGETATIVE CHARACTERISTICS:

Culms: dense clumps, 50-120 cm (20-47 in) tall, caespitose

Leaves: sheaths rounded; blades stiff, narrower than the sheath, involute upon drying, apex pungent

Ligules: ring of hairs, 1-1.5 mm (about 1/32 in) long, short

GROWTH CHARACTERISTICS:

forms extensive colonies of large bunches; flowers from April to September depending on warm temperatures and available moisture; reproduces by seeds and tillers

HABITAT:

grows best on moist, heavy clay soils; coastal flats and brackish marshes. Texas distribution: Areas 2, 6

Texas Range Plants

Eragrostis curvula
weeping lovegrass
(Gould, 1978)

WEEPING LOVEGRASS

Grass Family (Poaceae: Eragrosteae)

LATIN NAME:	*Eragrostis curvula* (Schrad.) Nees
LONGEVITY:	Perennial
SEASON:	Warm
ORIGIN:	Introduced
ECONOMIC VALUE:	Wildlife - poor Livestock - fair

This grass was given its common name for the way the many long, narrow, rolled leaves curve back toward the ground. The open panicle type seedhead is pyramid-shaped and not usually as wide as that of sand lovegrass. The leaf sheaths are not hairy.

FLORAL CHARACTERISTICS:

Inflorescence: panicle, 20-38 cm (8-15 in) long, 8-15 cm (3 1/8-6 in) wide, open, narrowly pyramidal; branches solitary or in pairs

Spikelets: 6-12 florets, gray-green, pedicel equal or shorter than spikelet; lemmas about 2.5 mm (3/32 in) long, obtuse, 3-nerved, nerves prominent

Awns: glumes, lemmas, and paleas awnless

Glumes: slightly unequal; first glume about 1.8 mm (1/16 in) long, acute; second glume about 2.8 mm (1/8 in) long, acute

VEGETATIVE CHARACTERISTICS:

Culms: caespitose, 60-150 cm (24-59 in) tall

Leaves: basal leaves droop back toward the ground; sheaths keeled, not pilose at the summit; blades elongate, 20-30 cm (8-12 in) long, 1-1.5 mm (1/32-1/16 in) wide, involute

Ligules: ring of hairs, 0.5-1 mm (1/32 in or less) long

GROWTH CHARACTERISTICS:

initiates growth in late spring, drought resistant; reproduces by seed and tillers

HABITAT:

introduced into sandy areas as a forage plant; persists along roadsides. Texas distribution: Areas 3-5, 7-9

Eragrostis intermedia
plains lovegrass
(Gould, 1951)

PLAINS LOVEGRASS

Grass Family (Poaceae: Eragrosteae)

LATIN NAME:	*Eragrostis intermedia* Hitchc.
LONGEVITY:	Perennial
SEASON:	Warm
ORIGIN:	Native
ECONOMIC VALUE:	Wildlife - fair Livestock - good

The seedhead of this lovegrass is oval in shape with fewer, smaller seed clusters than weeping or sand lovegrass. The plant is often smaller than weeping or sand lovegrass. Leaves are not rolled and not as wide as those of sand lovegrass. There are long, silky hairs in the axils of the lowermost branches of the seedhead.

FLORAL CHARACTERISTICS:

Inflorescence: panicle open, 20-40 cm (8-16 in) long, 15-25 cm (6-10 in) wide, ovate, pedicels longer than spikelets

Spikelets: ovate, 4-7 mm (5/32-1/4 in) long, 5-11 florets; lemmas leaf-like, 1.8-2.2 mm (about 1/16 in) long, narrowly lanceolate, green to reddish purple, 3-nerved, lateral nerves inconspicuous, gray-green

Awns: glumes, lemmas, and paleas awnless

Glumes: acute, leaf-like, unequal 1.2-2 mm (1/32-1/16 in) long

VEGETATIVE CHARACTERISTICS:

Culms: tufted, 50-80 cm (20-31 in) tall

Leaves: sheaths pilose at summit, otherwise glabrous; blades 15-20 cm (6-8 in) long, 2-4 mm (1/16-5/32 in) wide

Ligules: ciliate membrane, 0.1-0.2 mm (less than 1/64 in) long, minute

GROWTH CHARACTERISTICS:

starts growth in early spring; flowers June to November; reproduces by seeds and tillers

HABITAT:

primarily on dry, sandy, clayey, or rocky soils; often in disturbed sites. Texas distribution: Areas 2-7, 10

Eragrostis secundiflora
red lovegrass
(Gould and Box, 1965)

RED LOVEGRASS

Grass Family (Poaceae: Eragrosteae)

LATIN NAME: *Eragrostis secundiflora* Presl.

LONGEVITY: Perennial

SEASON: Warm

ORIGIN: Native

ECONOMIC VALUE: Wildlife - poor   Livestock - poor

This weedy grass does not resemble the other lovegrasses considered here. Although many specimens are red in color, the color is not a reliable characteristic. The seeds are borne on very short branches and are much larger than the other lovegrasses. The leaves are hairy at the top of the sheath and the blades short and flat.

FLORAL CHARACTERISTICS:

Inflorescence: panicle, loosely contracted to open, 5-25 cm (2-10 in) long, 3-12 cm (1 1/4-4 3/4 in) wide, spikelets in clusters along branches

Spikelets: short pedicellate, linear to ovate, laterally compressed, 5-18 mm (3/16-11/16 in) long, 3.5-5 mm (1/8-3/16 in) wide; 10-25 florets; lemmas 3-nerved, apex acute, reddish-purple tinge or blue-green

Awns: glumes, lemmas and paleas awnless

Glumes: glumes unequal, apex acute; first glume 2-3 mm (1/16-1/8 in) long, second glume 3-4 mm (1/8-5/32 in) long

VEGETATIVE CHARACTERISTICS:

Culms: tufted, 20-70 cm (8-28 in) tall, ascending

Leaves: sheaths pilose on margins near the apex, overlapping; blades, 7-12 cm (2 3/4-4 3/4 in) long, 2-3 mm (1/16-1/8 in) wide, flat

Ligules: ciliate membrane, 0.2-0.3 mm (less than 1/32 in) long

GROWTH CHARACTERISTICS:

flowers when moisture and temperatures are at adequate levels; reproduces by seeds and tillers

HABITAT:

generally in disturbed soils such as roadsides or overgrazed areas. Texas distribution: Areas 1-4, 6-9

Eragrostis trichodes
sand lovegrass
(plant, Gould, 1978)
(spikelet, Gould, 1975)

SAND LOVEGRASS

Grass Family (Poaceae: Eragrosteae)

LATIN NAME:	*Eragrostis trichodes* (Nutt.) Wood
LONGEVITY:	Perennial
SEASON:	Warm
ORIGIN:	Native
ECONOMIC VALUE:	Wildlife - poor Livestock - good

The diffuse seedhead of this grass is very large, often half the size of the entire plant. The flat leaves are wider than the other lovegrasses. The leaf sheaths are hairy at the top.

FLORAL CHARACTERISTICS:

Inflorescence: panicle, 35-55 cm (14-22 in) long, open, 7-30 cm (2 3/4-12 in) wide, diffuse, branches capillary, in whorls of 3-4; may be one half the plant height

Spikelets: 4-8 florets, spikelet 4-10 mm (5/32-3/8 in) long, pedicels long; lemmas 3-nerved, lateral nerves prominent

Awns: glumes, lemmas, and paleas awnless

Glumes: unequal, thin, pointed

VEGETATIVE CHARACTERISTICS:

Culms: erect, 40-180 cm (16-70 in) tall, caespitose

Leaves: sheaths pilose at the summit; blades elongate, 15-40 cm (6-16 in) long, 2-8 mm (1/16-5/16 in) wide, flat, scabrous

Ligules: ring of hairs, 0.2-0.5 mm (less than 1/32 in) long

GROWTH CHARACTERISTICS:

starts growth 2 or more weeks before other warm season grasses; reproduces by seeds and tillers

HABITAT:

deep sand or sandy loams. Texas distribution: Areas 1, 3-9

Erioneuron pilosum
hairy erioneuron
(Hitchcock, 1951)

HAIRY ERIONEURON

Grass Family (Poaceae: Eragrosteae)

LATIN NAME: *Erioneuron pilosum* (Buckl.) Nash

LONGEVITY: Perennial

SEASON: Warm

ORIGIN: Native

ECONOMIC VALUE: Wildlife - poor   Livestock - poor

Also commonly known as hairy tridens, this small grass is found throughout much of Texas. The small seedhead is densely hairy and may have very short awns. The short blunt-tipped leaves have white margins and are not hairy.

FLORAL CHARACTERISTICS:

Inflorescence: contracted panicle or raceme, 2-4 cm (3/4-1 1/2 in) long, with 3-10 large pale spikelets, 1-2 cm (3/8-3/4 in) wide

Spikelets: 7-14 florets; spikelet 10-15 mm (3/8-9/16 in) long; lemmas 3-nerved, nerves densely ciliate-pubescent, apex bifid with an awn

Awns: glumes awnless; lemma awn 1-2 mm (1/32-1/16 in) long; paleas awnless

Glumes: unequal, 1-nerved, 4-6 mm (5/32-1 1/4 in) long

VEGETATIVE CHARACTERISTICS:

Culms: tufted, 10-30 cm (4-12 in) long, erect to ascending

Leaves: mostly basal; sheaths keeled; blades flat, 2-10 cm (3/4-4 in) long, 1-3 mm (1/32-1/8 in) wide, glabrous, margins white, apex blunt

Ligules: ring of hairs, about 0.5 mm (less than 1/32 in) long

GROWTH CHARACTERISTICS:

flowers April to October depending on warm temperatures and adequate moisture; reproduces by seeds and tillers

HABITAT:

dry plains, rocky hillsides: Texas distribution: Areas 2, 4-10

Leptochloa dubia
green sprangletop
(Gould and Box, 1965)

GREEN SPRANGLETOP

Grass Family (Poaceae: Eragrosteae)

LATIN NAME:	*Leptochloa dubia* (H.B.K.) Nees
LONGEVITY:	Perennial
SEASON:	Warm
ORIGIN:	Native
ECONOMIC VALUE:	Wildlife - fair Livestock - good

The spreading, "sprangled" appearance of the seedhead gives this grass its common name. The groups of seeds lay close to the branches of the seedhead and each seed may appear notched at the tip. The leaves are rough on the upper surface. Peeling away a basal leaf sheath will often reveal hidden seeds at the base of the plant.

FLORAL CHARACTERISTICS:

Inflorescence: panicle of 2-16 spicate primary unilateral branches; branches 4-12 cm (1 1/2-4 3/4 in) long, usually alternate, usually spreading

Spikelets: 2-8 florets; short pedicelled; lemmas 3-nerved, emarginate to nearly truncate

Awns: glumes, lemmas, and paleas awnless

Glumes: unequal, lanceolate; first glume 3-4 mm (1/8-5/32 in) long; second glume 4-5 mm (5/32-3/16 in) long

VEGETATIVE CHARACTERISTICS:

Culms: erect, 30-100 cm (12-40 in) long, tufted, branched only at the base

Leaves: basal and cauline; sheaths keeled, flattened, glabrous to pilose; hair at collar 3-5 mm (1/8-3/16 in) long; basal sheaths with cleistogamous (hidden) spikelets

Ligules: ciliate membrane, about 0.5 mm (less than 1/32 in) long

GROWTH CHARACTERISTICS:

growth starts in April; reproduces by seeds, tillers, and rhizomes

HABITAT:

rocky hills and canyons, sandy soil. Texas distribution: Areas 2, 4-10

Texas Range Plants

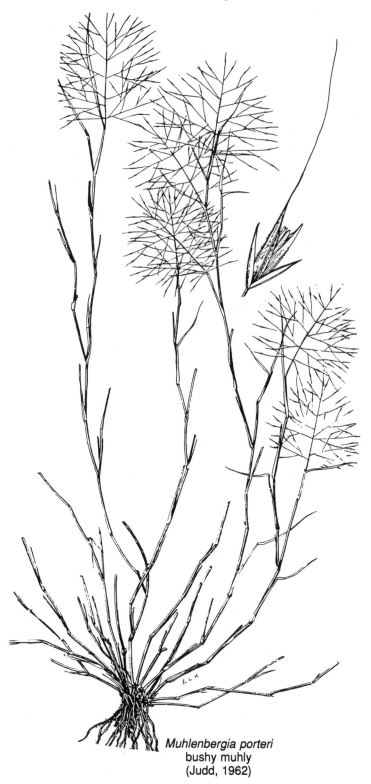

Muhlenbergia porteri
bushy muhly
(Judd, 1962)

BUSHY MUHLY

Grass Family (Poaceae: Eragrosteae)

LATIN NAME:	*Muhlenbergia porteri* Scribn. *ex* Beal
LONGEVITY:	Perennial
SEASON:	Warm
ORIGIN:	Native
ECONOMIC VALUE:	Wildlife - poor Livestock - good

This grass looks like a delicate bush because the stems branch often and are crooked and bent, appearing arthritic. The large open seedhead is characterized by awned seeds borne singly on delicate branches. The short leaves are flat and come to a point. The plant usually matures to a straw yellow color.

FLORAL CHARACTERISTICS:

Inflorescence: panicle, 4-14 cm (1 1/2-5 1/2 in) long, pyramidal, open

Spikelets: 3-4 mm (1/8-5/32 in) long, on pedicels 5-20 mm (3/16-3/4 in) long; lemma 3-nerved, sparsely pubescent; floret 1 per spikelet

Awns: glumes awnless; lemma awn delicate, 6-12 mm (1/4-1/2 in) long

Glumes: unequal, 2-3 mm (1/16-1/8 in) long, glabrous, acuminate

VEGETATIVE CHARACTERISTICS:

Culms: spreading, much branched, 30-60 cm (12-24 in) tall, branches wiry, geniculate from a woody base

Leaves: blades flat, 2-7 cm (3/4-2 3/4 in) long, 0.4-1.5 mm (less than 1/32-1/16 in) wide, pointed

Ligules: membranous, 1-2 mm (1/32-1/16 in) long, lacerate, truncate

GROWTH CHARACTERISTICS:

initiates growth in late spring or early summer, drought resistant, grows as a bushy bunchgrass under the protection of shrubs; reproduces by seeds, tillers, and short branched rhizomes

HABITAT:

adapted to sandy or dry rocky soil and along gullies and brushy flats. Texas distribution: Areas 7, 9, 10

Scleropogon brevifolius
burrograss
(Leithead, 1971)

BURROGRASS

Grass Family (Poaceae: Eragrosteae)

LATIN NAME: *Scleropogon brevifolius* Phil.

LONGEVITY: Perennial

SEASON: Warm

ORIGIN: Native

ECONOMIC VALUE: Wildlife - poor   Livestock - poor

Male and female plants of this grass grow in separate colonies, their seedheads are not at all alike. The leaves of both are short and strongly nerved. Female seedheads have three long, twisted awns per seed, but the seeds are larger than the threeawns. Male seedheads are awnless with pale, overlapping seeds.

FLORAL CHARACTERISTICS:

Inflorescence: panicle or spicate raceme, 1-7 cm (3/8-2 3/4 in) long, contracted

Spikelets: unisexual, staminate and pistillate spikelets dissimilar; staminate spikelets 2-3 cm (3/4-1 1/4 in) long, 5 to 20 florets; pistillate spikelets 2.5-3 cm (1-1 1/4 in) long, florets 3-5; lemma 3-nerved

Awns: glumes awnless; lemmas of pistillate spikelets with 3 awns, 5-10 cm (2-4 in) long, twisted; lemmas of staminate spikelets awnless

Glumes: staminate spikelet glumes thin, pale, separated by a short internode

VEGETATIVE CHARACTERISTICS:

Culms: tufted, 10-25 cm (4-10 in) tall stiffly erect; wiry creeping stolons

Leaves: basal; sheaths short, strongly nerved; blades flat or folded, 2-8 cm (3/4-3 1/8 in) long, 1-2 mm (1/32-1/16 in) wide, twisted

Ligules: ciliate membrane, 0.1-0.4 mm (less than 1/64 in) long, truncate

GROWTH CHARACTERISTICS:

plants dioecious; starts growth in May; reproduces by seeds, tillers, and stolons

HABITAT:

occurs in nearly pure stands; dry disturbed sites formerly supporting tobosa, usually on clayey soils. Texas distribution: Areas 7-10

Sporobolus airoides
alkali sacaton
(Hitchcock, 1951)

ALKALI SACATON

Grass Family (Poaceae: Eragrosteae)

LATIN NAME: *Sporobolus airoides* (Torr.) Torr.

LONGEVITY: Perennial

SEASON: Warm

ORIGIN: Native

ECONOMIC VALUE: Wildlife - poor   Livestock - fair

Stems of this tough bunchgrass spread slightly outward from the base of the plant. The seedhead is partially enclosed in the leaf sheath as it develops, but emerges completely at maturity. Tiny seeds are borne singly on branches in the loose, open seedhead. The top of the leaf sheath can have a ring of hairs, though these are not as long and dense as those of sand dropseed.

FLORAL CHARACTERISTICS:

Inflorescence: panicle, 20-50 cm (8-20 in) long, 20-30 cm (8-12 in) wide, pyramidal, open, usually not enclosed in the sheath; branches spreading, naked at the base; pedicels spreading, 0.5-2 mm (less than 1/32-1/16 in) long

Spikelets: 1 floret, 1.4-2.9 mm (1/32-1/8 in) long; lemma 1-nerved; palea occasionally splits into 2 parts

Awns: glumes, lemma, and palea awnless

Glumes: unequal, first glume one-half as long as the lemma; second glume 1.4-2.9 mm (1/32-1/8 in) long

VEGETATIVE CHARACTERISTICS:

Culms: erect, 0.5-1.3 m (20-51 in) tall; base hard, bleached, glabrous, shiny

Leaves: sheaths rounded, collar glabrous to sparsely pilose, hairs 2-4 mm (1/16-5/32 in) long; blades flat to involute, 5-50 cm (2-20 in) long, 2-6 mm (1/16-1/4 in) wide, tapering from base

Ligules: ciliate membrane, 0.5 mm (less than 1/32 in) long, hair to 5 mm (3/16 in) long

GROWTH CHARACTERISTICS:

withstands flooding; flowers April to September, seeds remain viable for many years; reproduces by seeds and tillers

HABITAT:

occurs in nearly pure stands on moist alkaline soils in valleys and meadows. Texas distribution: Areas 7-10

Sporobolus asper var. *drummondii*
meadow dropseed
(Gould, 1975)

MEADOW DROPSEED

Grass Family (Poaceae: Eragrosteae)

LATIN NAME:	*Sporobolus asper* (Michx.) Kunth var. *drummondii* (Trin.) Vasey
LONGEVITY:	Perennial
SEASON:	Warm
ORIGIN:	Native
ECONOMIC VALUE:	Wildlife - poor Livestock - fair

The leaves of this grass taper to a fine point and roll tightly at maturity. The seedhead is narrow compared to alkali sacaton and sand dropseed. It is usually at least partially, sometimes completely enclosed in the upper sheath. The seeds are larger than the other dropseeds included here.

FLORAL CHARACTERISTICS:

Inflorescence: panicle, 5-30 cm (2-12 in) long, 4-15 mm (5/32-9/16 in) wide, contracted, partially enclosed in an inflated sheath, solitary at the upper culm nodes; spikelets crowded

Spikelets: 1 floret; spikelet 3-7 mm (1/8-1/4 in) long; lemma 1-nerved, glabrous, apex somewhat rounded

Awns: glumes, lemmas, and paleas awnless

Glumes: unequal, keeled; first glume half the length of the lemma; second glume 2/3 to 3/4 the lemma length

VEGETATIVE CHARACTERISTICS:

Culms: erect, 60-120 cm (24-47 in) tall, slender, stout, solitary or in small tufts, occasionally with short rhizomes

Leaves: sheaths glabrous; blades 10-50 cm (4-20 in) long, 1-4 mm (1/32-5/32 in) wide, tapering to a fine point

Ligules: ciliate membrane, about 0.5 mm (less than 1/32 in) long, truncate

GROWTH CHARACTERISTICS:

starts growth in late spring, flowers in late August; reproduces by seeds, tillers, and some varieties also reproduce by rhizomes

HABITAT:

prairies or sandy meadows on silty to clay soils. Texas distribution: Areas 1-8

Sporobolus cryptandrus
sand dropseed
(Judd, 1962)

SAND DROPSEED

Grass Family (Poaceae: Eragrosteae)

LATIN NAME: *Sporobolus cryptandrus* (Torr.) Gray

LONGEVITY: Perennial

SEASON: Warm

ORIGIN: Native

ECONOMIC VALUE: Wildlife - poor   Livestock - fair

The most distinguishing feature of this grass are the long, dense hairs at the collar. The seedhead may be partially enclosed in the upper sheath or may be emerged and open, though not as open and spreading as alkali sacaton and not as slender as meadow dropseed. A distinct "flag-leaf" is usually present at a right angle to the stem, just below the seedhead.

FLORAL CHARACTERISTICS:

Inflorescence: contracted or pyramid-shaped panicle, 15-40 cm (6-16 in) long, 2-15 cm (3/4-6 in) wide; partially enclosed in sheath

Spikelets: 1 floret; spikelet 1.5-2.6 mm (1/32-1/8 in) long, crowded along the upper part of the branches; pedicels short; florets blunt; lemma 1-nerved

Awns: glumes, lemma, and palea awnless

Glumes: unequal, first glume about half the length of the second glume; second glume and lemma nearly the same length

VEGETATIVE CHARACTERISTICS:

Culms: erect, 30-120 cm (12-47 in) tall; some culms ascending

Leaves: sheaths rounded; collar pilose with hairs 2-4 mm (1/16-5/32 in) long; blades flat to involute, 4-35 cm (1 1/2-14 in) long, 2-8 mm (1/16-5/16 in) wide, tapering to a slender apex; flag leaf nearly at a right angle to the culm

Ligules: ciliate membrane, 0.5-3 mm (less than 1/32-1/8 in) long, rounded

GROWTH CHARACTERISTICS:

reproduces from small seeds and tillers; growth frequently controlled by available moisture

HABITAT:

common on sandy soils, occurs on rocky and silty soils. Texas distribution: Areas 2-10

Sporobolus indicus
rattail smutgrass
(Hitchcock, 1951)

RATTAIL SMUTGRASS

Grass Family (Poaceae: Eragrosteae)

LATIN NAME: *Sporobolus indicus* (L.) R. Br.

LONGEVITY: Perennial

SEASON: Warm

ORIGIN: Introduced

ECONOMIC VALUE: Wildlife - poor   Livestock - poor

Another of the "dropseeds", the seedhead of this grass is long and slender, resembling a rat's tail. Frequently the many tiny seeds are infested with a black fungus, hence the name "smutgrass".

FLORAL CHARACTERISTICS:

Inflorescence: contracted panicle, 10-35 cm (4-14 in) long; branches ascending about 2 cm (3/4 in) long, densely flowered

Spikelets: 1 floret, spikelet 1.5-2 mm (about 1/16 in) long; lemmas 1-nerved, 1.4-1.9 mm (about 1/16 in) long, glabrous; palea same texture as lemma and nearly as long

Awns: glumes, lemma, and palea awnless

Glumes: unequal, thin, 1-nerved; first glume one-half spikelet length; second glume one-half to two-thirds the length

VEGETATIVE CHARACTERISTICS:

Culms: erect, 30-90 cm (12-35 in) tall, glabrous, tough

Leaves: mostly basal; blades flat or folded or involute, 10-30 cm (4-12 in) long, 1-5 mm (1/32-3/16 in) wide, tapering to a flexuous tip

Ligules: ciliate membrane, 0.2-0.5 mm (less than 1/32 in) long

GROWTH CHARACTERISTICS:

flowers March to December under favorable conditions; rank throughout the year; reproduces by seeds and tillers

HABITAT:

moist clay and sands of disturbed sites. Texas distribution: 1-4, 7

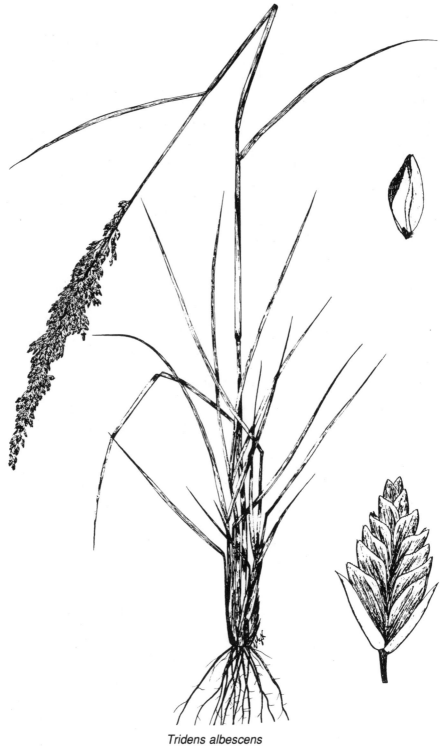

Tridens albescens
white tridens
(Gould and Box, 1965)

WHITE TRIDENS

Grass Family (Poaceae: Eragrosteae)

LATIN NAME:	*Tridens albescens* (Vasey) Woot. & Standl.
LONGEVITY:	Perennial
SEASON:	Warm
ORIGIN:	Native
ECONOMIC VALUE:	Wildlife - fair Livestock - fair

This grass typically has few stems that form a loose tuft. It has both basal leaves and leaves up along the stem. The leaves are rough on the upper surface and taper to a point. The seedhead appears spike-like with small stacks of seeds borne in V-shaped bracts (glumes). The seeds are often white with a reddish tinge.

FLORAL CHARACTERISTICS:

Inflorescence: panicle, 7-20 cm (2 3/4-8 in) long, contracted; branches short and appressed, 1-5 cm (3/8-2 in) long, pedicels 2-8 mm (1/16-5/16 in) long

Spikelets: 4-10 florets; lemma 3-4 mm (1/8-5/32 in) long, thin, 3-nerved, nerves nearly glabrous, yellow or with purple near the apex

Awns: glumes awnless, lemmas mucronate, paleas awnless

Glumes: glume nearly equal, 1-nerved, acute

VEGETATIVE CHARACTERISTICS:

Culms: tufted, 30-80 cm (12-31 in) tall, glabrous; base often knotty or rhizomatous

Leaves: basal and cauline; sheaths glabrous, lower ones keeled, upper ones rounded; blades 1-4 mm (1/32-5/32 in) wide, glaucous, glabrous, apex attenuate

Ligules: ciliate membrane, to 0.5 mm or less (less than 1/32 in) long

GROWTH CHARACTERISTICS:

flowers March to November; plants may have sour odor; reproduces from seeds, tillers, and rhizomes

HABITAT:

clayey soil of wet areas, ditches, or swales. Texas distribution: Areas 2-10

Tridens flavus
purpletop
(Hitchcock, 1951)

PURPLETOP

Grass Family (Poaceae: Eragrosteae)

LATIN NAME:	*Tridens flavus* (L.) Hitchc.
LONGEVITY:	Perennial
SEASON:	Warm
ORIGIN:	Native
ECONOMIC VALUE:	Wildlife - fair Livestock - fair

A large, robust perennial bunchgrass with wide, flat leaf blades. The purple seedhead is pyramidal and drooping, and frequently covered with an oily substance. This oily substance on the branches has caused some people to call this grass "greasegrass". Plant mounts of purpletop often have dirt clinging to the oily substance on the seedhead branches.

FLORAL CHARACTERISTICS:

Inflorescence: panicle, 12-35 cm (4 3/4-14 in) long, open; branches 10-25 cm (4-10 in) long, widely spreading, base of branches without spikelets for one-third the length or more

Spikelets: short pediceled, 5-9 mm (3/16-11/32 in) long; 4-7 florets, clustered near the branch tips; lemmas 3-nerved, 3-5 mm (1/8-3/16 in) long, firm, lateral nerves pubescent to ciliate on the lower half, apex notched and slightly mucronate

Awns: glumes awnless to mucronate; lemmas mucronate; paleas awnless

Glumes: unequal, 1-nerved, acute to obtuse

VEGETATIVE CHARACTERISTICS:

Culms: caespitose, 60-150 cm (24-59 in) tall, glabrous

Leaves: sheaths pubescent at the collar, lower sheaths keeled; blades elongate, 3-10 mm (1/8-3/8 in) wide, attenuate, glabrous

Ligules: ciliate membrane, 0.2-0.5 mm (less than 1/32 in) long

GROWTH CHARACTERISTICS:

shade tolerant, flowers August to November; reproduces by seeds and tillers

HABITAT:

open woods and roadsides. Texas distribution: Areas 1-5, 7, 8

Axonopus affinis
common carpetgrass
(Gould and Box, 1965)

COMMON CARPETGRASS

Grass Family (Poaceae: Paniceae)

LATIN NAME: *Axonopus affinis* Chase

LONGEVITY: Perennial

SEASON: Warm

ORIGIN: Native

ECONOMIC VALUE: Wildlife - fair   Livestock - fair

This grass may be tufted or spreading but nearly always occupies a moist habitat. The seedhead most often consists of two paired branches, perhaps with a third or fourth below. These branches are ascending, not divergent. Leaf blades are blunt at the apex.

FLORAL CHARACTERISTICS:

Inflorescence: panicle of 2-4 spicate primary unilateral branches; branches spreading at the culm apex, 2-7 cm (3/4-2 3/4 in) long, each with two rows of appressed spikelets

Spikelets: 2 florets; spikelet about 2-2.5 mm (1/16-3/32 in) long; lower lemma oblong, sparsely pubescent; lemma of upper floret minutely rugose, perfect

Awns: glumes, lemmas, and paleas awnless

Glumes: first glume absent; second glume about spikelet length

VEGETATIVE CHARACTERISTICS:

Culms: erect, 20-60 cm (8-24 in) tall, glabrous, tufted, flattened, caespitose or stoloniferous

Leaves: glabrous on both surfaces; sheaths sparsely ciliate near margins; blades 1.5-7 mm (1/32-1/4 in) wide, sparsely ciliate near ligule

Ligules: ciliate membrane, 0.1-0.2 mm (less than 1/64 in) long, minute

GROWTH CHARACTERISTICS:

occurs in nearly pure stands; flowers from April to December, depending on warm temperatures and moisture; reproduces by seeds, tillers, and stolons

HABITAT:

adapted to slightly acid soils; moist, sandy woods openings or stream borders. Texas distribution: Areas 1-3

Cenchrus ciliaris
buffelgrass
(Gould and Box, 1965)

BUFFELGRASS

Grass Family (Poaceae: Paniceae)

LATIN NAME: *Cenchrus ciliaris* L.

LONGEVITY: Perennial

SEASON: Warm

ORIGIN: Introduced

ECONOMIC VALUE: Wildlife - poor   Livestock - good

This midgrass was introduced to Texas as a forage species and has adapted to many sites. Freely branching stems arise from a "knotty" base. It is characterized by purple, bristly seedheads. Each seed is surrounded by numerous bristles which are more delicate than those of big cenchrus.

FLORAL CHARACTERISTICS:

Inflorescence: dense spicate panicle, 3-14 cm (1 1/4-5 1/2 in) long, 1-2 cm (3/8-3/4 in) wide

Spikelets: in groups of 2-4, subtended and enclosed by numerous bristles; bristles 4-10 mm (5/32-3/8 in) long, purple, ciliate on margins; spikelets 2.2-5.6 mm (1/16-1/4 in) long, 2 florets

Awns: glumes, lemmas, and paleas awnless

Glumes: first glume acute, one-third the length of the spikelet; second glume acute, equals spikelet length

VEGETATIVE CHARACTERISTICS:

Culms: erect or spreading, 30-110 cm (12-43 in) tall, branching

Leaves: sheaths keeled, glabrous to pilose; blades thin, flat, 7-26 cm (2 3/4-10 in) long

Ligules: ciliate membrane, 1-1.5 mm (1/32-1/16 in) long

GROWTH CHARACTERISTICS:

initiates growth in late spring, lacks cold tolerance, most productive when fertilized; reproduces by seeds, tillers, and rhizomes

HABITAT:

adapted to fine-coarse textured soils, native to Africa and India, planted extensively in South Texas following mechanical brush control. Texas distribution: Areas 2, 3, 6, 7, 10

Cenchrus myosuroides
big cenchrus
(bur and spikelet, Gould and Box, 1965)

BIG CENCHRUS

Grass Family (Poaceae: Paniceae)

LATIN NAME: *Cenchrus myosuroides* H.B.K.

LONGEVITY: Perennial

SEASON: Warm

ORIGIN: Native

ECONOMIC VALUE: Wildlife - fair   Livestock - good

This large, coarse, perennial bunchgrass occurs in large clumps. Stems are nearly woody with little branching. Leaves are flat to somewhat folded. Seedheads are bristly and spike-like. Seeds are covered with spines and bristles that stick to anything they touch.

FLORAL CHARACTERISTICS:

Inflorescence: spicate panicle 6-14 cm (2 3/8-5 1/2 in) long, tightly contracted, with 1 spikelet per bur on a short branch or subsessile

Spikelets: spines and bristles subtend and encircle spikelet forming a bur, retrosely scabrous; spikelet 4-5 mm (5/32-3/16 in) long; 2 florets, upper floret fertile

Awns: glumes, lemmas, and paleas awnless

Glumes: first glume acute, second as long as the spikelet

VEGETATIVE CHARACTERISTICS:

Culms: 1-1.5 m (39-59 in) tall, in large clumps, with smooth woody stems, decumbent at base; nodes swollen

Leaves: blades scabrous on upper surface, 10-35 cm (4-14 in) long, flat or folded, 5-12 mm (3/16-7/16 in) wide

Ligules: ciliate membrane, 1-3 mm (1/32-1/8 in) long

GROWTH CHARACTERISTICS:

growth initiated in spring, flowering from May to November; reproduces by seed and tillers

HABITAT:

grows on sandy to clay soils along ditches, streams, and gullies. Texas distribution: Areas 2, 6, 7, 10

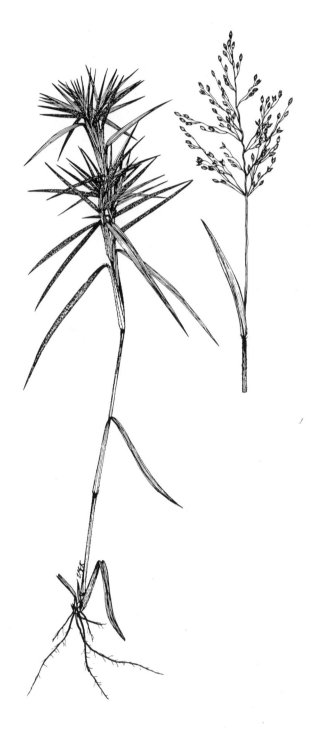

Dichanthelium oligosanthes var. *scribnerianum*
scribner rosettegrass
(Gould and Box, 1965)

SCRIBNER ROSETTEGRASS

Grass Family (Poaceae: Paniceae)

LATIN NAME: *Dichanthelium oligosanthes* (Schult.) Gould
                            var. *scribnerianum* (Nash) Gould

LONGEVITY: Perennial

SEASON: Cool

ORIGIN: Native

ECONOMIC VALUE: Wildlife - fair   Livestock - fair

A relatively short grass from a basal rosette of winter leaves. Base of the leaf has long stiff hairs. The seedhead of the plants growing in the spring has an open branching pattern with round seeds. Seedheads of summer or fall flowering plants have very few seeds included in the clusters of leaves.

FLORAL CHARACTERISTICS:

Inflorescence: panicle, 4-12 cm (1 1/2-4 3/4 in) long, open, narrowly pyramidal, well-exserted; fall inflorescence not-well exserted with less than 12 spikelets, axillary

Spikelets: blunt; 2 florets; spikelet elliptic to obovate, 2.5-3.8 mm (3/32-5/32 in) long, glabrous

Awns: glumes, lemmas and paleas awnless

Glumes: first glume 0.8-2.2 mm (1/32-1/16 in) long; second glume 2.5-3.8 mm (3/32-5/32 in) long

VEGETATIVE CHARACTERISTICS:

Culms: erect, 20-60 cm (8-24 in) tall, glabrous

Leaves: basal rosette of short blades; sheaths glabrous to hispid; blades 3-13 cm (1 1/4-5 1/8 in) long, 3-14 mm (1/8-1/2 in) wide

Ligules: fringe of hairs, 0.1-1/6 mm (less than 1/32-1/16 in) long

GROWTH CHARACTERISTICS:

flowers April to June and again when moisture is readily available in the fall; reproduces by seeds and tillers

HABITAT:

loam to clay loam soils on prairies in open or brushy sites. Texas distribution: Areas 1-10

Digitaria californica
Arizona cottontop
(Judd, 1962)

ARIZONA COTTONTOP

Grass Family (Poaceae: Paniceae)

LATIN NAME:	*Digitaria californica* (Benth.) Henr.
LONGEVITY:	Perennial
SEASON:	Warm
ORIGIN:	Native
ECONOMIC VALUE:	Wildlife - fair Livestock - good

Perennial bunchgrass from a swollen hairy base. Basal sheaths are hairy. Leaves are flat and narrow. Seedheads are narrow to open having several branches with long white or purplish hairs. The margins of the seeds are covered with long hairs. The cottony appearance of the seeds has resulted in the common name. It is also often referred to as California cottontop.

FLORAL CHARACTERISTICS:

Inflorescence: panicle, 8-20 cm (3 1/8-8 in) long, erect, contracted to narrow; branches 3-6 cm (1 1/4-2 3/8 in) long, alternate, ascending, racemose

Spikelets: paired; 2 florets; covered with white to purple silky hairs that exceed the spikelet length

Awns: glumes awnless; upper lemma mucronate; paleas awnless

Glumes: first glume minute, glabrous; second glume densely villous, as long as the spikelet

VEGETATIVE CHARACTERISTICS:

Culms: erect, 40-100 cm (16-39 in) tall; base knotty, swollen, often purplish

Leaves: lowermost sheaths pubescent to hairy; blades 2-15 cm (3/4-6 in) long, 2-8 mm (1/16-5/16 in) wide, pubescent, glandular on lower surface

Ligules: membranous, 1.5-2.5 mm (about 1/16 in) long, outline rounded, erose to lacerate

GROWTH CHARACTERISTICS:

starts growth in April or when adequate temperature and moisture are available; reproduces by seeds and tillers

HABITAT:

adapted to gravelly and sandy loam soils; chaparral, desert shrub, desert grassland and dry plains. Texas distribution: Areas 2, 4-10

Texas Range Plants

Digitaria cognata
fall witchgrass
(Gould and Box, 1965)

FALL WITCHGRASS

Grass Family (Poaceae: Paniceae)

LATIN NAME: *Digitaria cognata* (Schult.) Pilger
                  (*Leptoloma cognatum* (Schult.) Chase)

LONGEVITY: Perennial

SEASON: Warm

ORIGIN: Native

ECONOMIC VALUE: Wildlife - fair   Livestock - fair

A short grass with a diffuse seedhead and relatively small, awnless seeds. The seedhead is nearly as wide as it is long. Leaf blade is typically "crinkled" on one margin.

FLORAL CHARACTERISTICS:

Inflorescence: panicle, 10-40 cm (4-16 in) long, 10-40 cm (4-16 in) wide, open; disarticulates at base and becomes a "tumbleweed"; pedicels long, spreading

Spikelets: 2 florets, spikelet 2.5-4 mm (3/32-5/32 in) long; lower lemma staminate, villous between nerves and glabrous near margins; upper lemma dark brown, smooth, acute at apex, thin flat margins

Awns: glumes, lemmas, and paleas awnless

Glumes: first glume absent or vestigial; second glume well-developed

VEGETATIVE CHARACTERISTICS:

Culms: knotty, felty pubescent, 20-60 cm (8-24 in) tall, erect to ascending; some taxa with rhizomes

Leaves: sheaths rounded; blades short, flat, crisp on one or both margins near the base

Ligules: membranous, 0.5 mm (less than 1/32 in) long, truncate

GROWTH CHARACTERISTICS:

flowers May to November; reproduces from seeds, tillers, and rhizomes

HABITAT:

sandy or clay soils of prairies and plains. Texas distribution: Areas 1-10

Echinochloa crusgalli var. *crusgalli*
barnyardgrass
(Hitchcock, 1951)

BARNYARDGRASS

Grass Family (Poaceae: Paniceae)

LATIN NAME: *Echinochloa crusgalli* (L.) Beauv. var. *crusgalli*

LONGEVITY: Annual

SEASON: Warm

ORIGIN: Introduced

ECONOMIC VALUE: Wildlife - poor   Livestock - poor

This weedy annual varies greatly in size. The seeds may have many awns, few awns, or be awnless. The awn lengths may vary as well. The Latin name "Echinochloa" means hedgehog-grass" and refers to the seeds of barnyardgrass which are covered with bulbous-based hairs and resemble a hedgehog.

FLORAL CHARACTERISTICS:

Inflorescence: panicle, 9-26 cm (3 1/2-10 in) long, with 5-20 appressed to slightly spreading branches, branches frequently rebranched

Spikelets: ovate or elliptic, 2.8-4 mm (3/32-5/32 in) long; glabrous to hirsute; 2 florets; lower floret with a well-developed palea; lemma of upper floret obtuse with a withering membranous apex

Awns: second glume short-awned; lemma of lower floret awnless or short awned, over 5 cm (2 in) long

Glumes: first glume half the length of second glume, acute; second glume as long as spikelet, pubescent

VEGETATIVE CHARACTERISTICS:

Culms: erect, 30-90 cm (12-35 in) tall, glabrous, nodes swollen

Leaves: sheaths glabrous; blades scabrous to hirsute, to 40 cm (16 in) long

Ligules: absent

GROWTH CHARACTERISTICS:

initiates growth in mid-spring, flowers July to November; reproduces by seeds

HABITAT:

adapted to disturbed sites, roadsides, field borders, and ditches, in wet areas. Texas distribution: Areas 1-10

Eriochloa sericea
Texas cupgrass
(Gould and Box, 1965)

TEXAS CUPGRASS

Grass Family (Poaceae: Paniceae)

LATIN NAME: *Eriochloa sericea* (Scheele) Munro

LONGEVITY: Perennial

SEASON: Warm

ORIGIN: Native

ECONOMIC VALUE: Wildlife - fair   Livestock - good

This tufted grass often has may leaves but comparatively few slender stems. The stems are hairy just below the seedhead and may have hairs scattered elsewhere. The seeds are pressed tightly to the branch of the seedhead and each seed appears to be set into a small cup, hence the common name.

FLORAL CHARACTERISTICS:

Inflorescence: panicle, 4-20 cm (1 1/2-8 in) long, narrow, with few branches; branches 1.5-3 cm (9/16-1 1/4 in) long, hirsute, appressed

Spikelets: about 4 mm (5/32 in) long; 2 florets, ovate, pubescent; upper floret perfect, 3 mm (1/8 in) long

Awns: second glume awnless; upper lemma mucronate

Glumes: first glume reduces to cup-like ring or disk below the second glume; second glume hirsute

VEGETATIVE CHARACTERISTICS:

Culms: tufted, 50-90 cm (20-35 in) tall, erect to ascending; nodes pubescent

Leaves: lower sheaths pubescent, upper sheaths glabrous; blades 2-3 mm (1/16-1/8 in) wide, elongate, flat or involute

Ligules: ciliate membrane, about 1 mm (1/32 in) long

GROWTH CHARACTERISTICS:

flowers April to November; does not withstand heavy grazing; reproduces by seeds and tillers

HABITAT:

prairies and opening in shrublands. Texas distribution: Areas 2, 4-8

Panicum anceps
beaked panicum
(Gould, 1975)

BEAKED PANICUM

Grass Family (Poaceae: Paniceae)

LATIN NAME: *Panicum anceps* Michx.

LONGEVITY: Perennial

SEASON: Warm

ORIGIN: Native

ECONOMIC VALUE: Wildlife - fair   Livestock - good

A prolific seed producer, this rhizomatous grass has a seed that resembles the slightly curved beak of a bird, hence the common name. Leaf blades are folded and hairy near the base. Most often found in moist to wet soils of partially shaded habitats.

FLORAL CHARACTERISTICS:

Inflorescence: panicle, 12-30 cm (4 3/4-12 in) long, open, spikelets on short pedicels, clustered

Spikelets: glabrous, 2.8-3.4 mm (about 1/8 in) long; 2 florets, lemma of lower floret acute; upper floret shorter than second glume, indurate (seedlike), perfect and fertile

Awns: glumes, lemmas, and paleas awnless

Glumes: first glume half as long as the second glume; second glume is curved like a birds beak, as long as spikelet

VEGETATIVE CHARACTERISTICS:

Culms: erect, 50-120 cm (20-47 in) tall, with weak rhizomes

Leaves: sheaths keeled, tinged with soft purple hairs; blades folded or keeled, over 1 cm (3/8 in) wide; upper surface pubescent; leaves ascending

Ligules: membranous, 0.1-0.2 mm (less than 1/64 in) long, minute

GROWTH CHARACTERISTICS:

starts growth in February, stays green year round, inflorescences are produced in the fall, tolerant of shade and moisture; reproduces by seeds, tillers, and rhizomes

HABITAT:

grows best in moist wet soils and shade. Texas distribution: Areas 1-4

Panicum antidotale
blue panicum
(Gould and Box, 1965)

BLUE PANICUM

Grass Family (Poaceae: Paniceae)

LATIN NAME: *Panicum antidotale* Retz.

LONGEVITY: Perennial

SEASON: Warm

ORIGIN: Introduced

ECONOMIC VALUE: Wildlife - good   Livestock - good (poisonous)

This stout, tall plant is often a distinctive light green color. The seeds are very slick and shiny, yellow-green in color. The stems may branch at the nodes. The leaves have a prominent midrib on the underside and are often wavy on both leaf margins. Plants may cause nitrate poisoning when animals are grazed on fertilized pastures.

FLORAL CHARACTERISTICS:

Inflorescence: panicle, 20-30 cm (8-12 in) long, open, spikelets on short pedicels

Spikelets: glabrous, ovate, 2.5-3 mm (1/16-1/8 in) long; 2 florets; lower floret staminate with long palea; upper floret hard, shiny, as long as spikelet, fertile

Awns: glumes, lemmas, and paleas awnless

Glumes: first glume one-third to one-half length of spikelet, rounded to obtuse; second glume as long as spikelet

VEGETATIVE CHARACTERISTICS:

Culms: hard, bush-like with age, 50-200 cm (20-79 in) tall, from short rhizomes; basal nodes appear double, swollen

Leaves: sheath glabrous; blades flat, glabrous to puberulent, 4-11 mm (5/32-1/2 in) wide

Ligules: ciliate membrane, 0.5-1 mm (less than 1/32 in) long

GROWTH CHARACTERISTICS:

initiates growth in late spring; requires fertilization and irrigation to retain vigor; reproduces by seeds, tillers, and rhizomes

HABITAT:

adapted to a variety of soils, particularly clay loam soils. Texas distribution: Areas 2-4, 6-9

Panicum coloratum
kleingrass
(Gould, 1978)

KLEINGRASS

Grass Family (Poaceae: Paniceae)

LATIN NAME: *Panicum coloratum* L.

LONGEVITY: Perennial

SEASON: Warm

ORIGIN: Introduced

ECONOMIC VALUE: Wildlife - fair   Livestock - good (poisonous)

While beaked panicum has scaly rhizomes, this panicum has a knotty base. Stem nodes are often dark in color. Leaves and leaf sheaths may have glandular based hairs. Kleingrass has comparatively fewer seeds than beaked or blue panicum. A fungal association with kleingrass causes hepatic photosensitization in sheep and goats.

FLORAL CHARACTERISTICS:

Inflorescence: panicle, 7-20 cm (2 3/4-8 in) long, spikelets on short pedicels

Spikelets: glabrous, 2.6-3.1 mm (about 1/8 in) long; 2 florets; lower floret staminate, with a long palea; upper floret fertile, glabrous, shiny, hard, with acute apex

Awns: glumes, lemmas, and paleas awnless

Glumes: first glume broad at base with an acute apex, 1-1.5 mm (about 1/32 in) long; second glume as long as spikelet

VEGETATIVE CHARACTERISTICS:

Culms: erect, 50-120 cm (20-47 in) tall, from a knotty base

Leaves: sheaths glabrous or with papillose based hairs; blades 2.5 mm (1/16-3/16 in) wide, with scattered papillose based hairs on margins

Ligules: a ciliate membrane, 0.5-2 mm (less than 1/32-1/16 in) long

GROWTH CHARACTERISTICS:

initiates growth in late spring, good to fair drought tolerance, poor cold tolerance; may require fertilization and irrigation for vigorous forage production; reproduces by seeds and tillers

HABITAT:

adapted to a variety of soils especially sand-clay and a variety of climates. Texas distribution: Area 7

Panicum hallii var. *hallii*
Hall panicum
(Gould and Box, 1965)

HALL PANICUM

Grass Family (Poaceae: Paniceae)

LATIN NAME:	*Panicum hallii* Vasey var. *hallii*
LONGEVITY:	Perennial
SEASON:	Warm
ORIGIN:	Native
ECONOMIC VALUE:	Wildlife - fair Livestock - fair

This grass is easily recognized at maturity or when dried by the curling basal leaves. The straw yellow color and characteristic curling of the leaves makes them resemble wood shavings. The leaves have no hair. The hard, shiny seeds are borne on spreading branches.

FLORAL CHARACTERISTICS:

Inflorescence: panicle with few branches, outline pyramidal, spikelets with short pedicels

Spikelets: glabrous, acute, 2.2-3.6 mm (1/16-5/32 in) long, over 1 mm (1/32 in) wide; 2 florets; upper floret dark brown, shiny and hard, fertile

Awns: glumes, lemmas, and paleas awnless

Glumes: first glume acute, one-third to two-thirds the length of the spikelet; second glume as long as spikelet

VEGETATIVE CHARACTERISTICS:

Culms: erect, 15-70 cm (6-28 in) tall, nodes glabrous to pubescent

Leaves: glaucous; blades flat, curling upon drying

Ligules: a ciliate membrane, to 1.5 mm (about 1/16 in) long

GROWTH CHARACTERISTICS:

initiates growth in early spring, flowers from April to November; reproduces by seeds and tillers

HABITAT:

adapted to sand or clay soils, particularly calcareous soils, this variety occurs on dry, arid sites. Texas distribution: Areas 2-10

Panicum obtusum
vinemesquite
(Judd, 1962)

VINEMESQUITE

Grass Family (Poaceae: Paniceae)

LATIN NAME: *Panicum obtusum* H.B.K.

LONGEVITY: Perennial

SEASON: Warm

ORIGIN: Native

ECONOMIC VALUE: Wildlife - fair   Livestock - good

The stolons of this grass may grow several feet long and have swollen woolly nodes. The brownish, round seeds lie close to the main seed stem forming a narrow seedhead. Often one leaf clings closely to the seedhead.

FLORAL CHARACTERISTICS:

Inflorescence: panicle, 3-15 cm (1 1/4-6 in) long, 5-14 mm (3/16-1/2 in) wide; branches erect, distant, usually unbranched

Spikelets: 2 florets, spikelet obovate, 3-4 mm (1/8-5/32 in) long, glabrous, brown at maturity; upper floret indurate, glabrous, brownish

Awns: glumes, lemmas, and paleas awnless

Glumes: first and second glume nearly as long as spikelet, apex of both obtuse

VEGETATIVE CHARACTERISTICS:

Culms: erect, 20-60 cm (8-24 in) tall, from a knotty or rhizomatous or stoloniferous base

Leaves: sheaths rounded with glandular papilla-based hairs; collar hairy, sometimes pilose on margins; blades firm, 5-20 cm (2-8 in) long, 2-8 mm (1/16-5/16 in) wide

Ligules: membranous, 1-2 mm (1/32-1/16 in) long, apex erose

GROWTH CHARACTERISTICS:

initiates growth in April to May; frequently grows in almost pure stands; withstands heavy grazing; reproduces by seeds, tillers, stolons, and rhizomes

HABITAT:

sandy or gravelly or clayey soils in areas of moisture accumulation. Texas distribution: Areas 2-10

Panicum virgatum
switchgrass
(Hitchcock, 1951)

SWITCHGRASS

Grass Family (Poaceae: Paniceae)

LATIN NAME: *Panicum virgatum* L.

LONGEVITY: Perennial

SEASON: Warm

ORIGIN: Native

ECONOMIC VALUE: Wildlife - fair   Livestock - good

This tall, robust bunchgrass is another of the important components of the True Prairies. The seedhead is large and pyramid-shaped, open with seeds borne on the tips of the branches. When open and mature, the seeds resemble a "W". Large, flat leaves have a triangular patch of hair near the base. The plant is strongly rhizomatous.

FLORAL CHARACTERISTICS:

Inflorescence: panicle, 15-60 cm (6-24 in) long, outline obovate, diffuse; lower nodes with branches in whorls

Spikelets: 2 florets, lower floret sterile or staminate, upper floret perfect and fertile; upper lemma 3-5 mm (1/8-3/16 in) long, smooth and shiny, margins clasp the palea

Awns: glumes, lemmas, and paleas awnless

Glumes: unequal, acute to acuminate; first glume three-fourths the length of the second, encircles the base of the second glume

VEGETATIVE CHARACTERISTICS:

Culms: erect, 50-300 cm (20 in-10 ft) tall, robust, with short rhizomes

Leaves: sheaths rounded, often red to purplish at base; blades 10-60 cm (10-24 in) long, 3-15 mm (1/8-9/16 in) wide, flat, elongate, adaxial surface at the blade base with a triangular patch of hair

Ligules: ciliate membrane, 1.5-3.5 mm (1/32-5/32 in) long, apex truncate to rounded

GROWTH CHARACTERISTICS:

adapted to withstand below freezing temperatures for extended periods; starts growth in April; reproduces from seeds, rhizomes, and tillers

HABITAT:

moist to mesic prairie sites, brackish marsh margins, pinewoods, and savannahs. Texas distribution: Areas 1-10

Paspalum dilatatum
dallisgrass
(Hitchcock, 1951)

DALLISGRASS

Grass Family (Poaceae: Paniceae)

LATIN NAME:	*Paspalum dilatatum* Poir.
LONGEVITY:	Perennial
SEASON:	Warm
ORIGIN:	Introduced
ECONOMIC VALUE:	Wildlife - fair Livestock - good

Stems of this grass are usually spreading widely from a leafy base with short rhizomes. Near the base of the plant, the stem nodes are often swollen and dark. There are usually two or three branches in the seedhead. These appear to bear four rows of seeds along one side of the branch. Resembling tomato seeds, the seeds are flattened and covered with silky white hairs.

FLORAL CHARACTERISTICS:

Inflorescence: panicle of 2-5 racemose branches; branches 3-10 cm (1 1/4-4 in) long; spikelets in 4 rows on one side of branches

Spikelets: solitary, flattened on one side; fringed with silky hairs; 2 florets

Awns: glume, lemmas, and paleas awnless

Glumes: first glume absent; second glume 3-4 mm (1/8-5/32 in) long, 3-5-nerved

VEGETATIVE CHARACTERISTICS:

Culms: erect, 50-120 cm (20-47 in) tall, tufted, knotty, base geniculate, short rhizomes

Leaves: basal and cauline; lower sheaths pubescent to hirsute, upper sheaths glabrous; blades flat, 10-30 cm (4-12 in) long, 3-12 mm (1/8-1/2 in) wide, tapering from the base, glabrous to ciliate

Ligules: membranous, 1-3 mm (1/32-1/8 in) long, rounded, entire, brown

GROWTH CHARACTERISTICS:

starts growth in March to April, drought tolerant; reproduces by seeds, tillers, and rhizomes

HABITAT:

lower areas, dry prairies, waste places and disturbed sites; seeded as a pasture grass. Texas distribution: Areas 1-6, 8, 10

Paspalum lividum
longtoms
(Gould and Box, 1965)

LONGTOM

Grass Family (Poaceae: Paniceae)

LATIN NAME: *Paspalum lividum* Trin.

LONGEVITY: Perennial

SEASON: Warm

ORIGIN: Native

ECONOMIC VALUE: Wildlife - fair   Livestock - fair

A stoloniferous grass with flattened sheaths. The leaves are comparatively shorter than the other Paspalum species considered here. The seedhead has several (3-7) short branches with seeds arranged in several rows along one side of the branch. The branches are the shortest of the paspalums with straw-colored seeds that appear wrinkled. Tolerates moderate salinity and inundation for long periods.

FLORAL CHARACTERISTICS:

Inflorescence: panicle of 3-7 spreading to erect, racemose branches; branches 1.5-5 cm (5/8-2 in) long, often becoming dark purple; spikelets in 4 rows on one side of the branch

Spikelets: glabrous, elliptical to obovate, 2-2.5 mm (1/16-3/32 in) long; 2 florets; lemma of upper floret wrinkled, straw colored, fertile

Awns: glume, lemmas, and paleas awnless

Glumes: first glume absent; second glume thin, nearly as long as spikelet

VEGETATIVE CHARACTERISTICS:

Culms: flattened, 30-60 cm (12-24 in) tall, decumbent or stoloniferous, stolons often to 1 m (39 in) long

Leaves: lower sheaths keeled; blades glabrous, 3-6 mm (1/8-1/4 in) wide

Ligules: membranous, 1.5-1.8 mm (less than 1/16 in) long, short

GROWTH CHARACTERISTICS:

growth initiated in early spring remaining green until frost; inflorescences produced late summer or fall; reproduces from seeds, tillers, and stolons

HABITAT:

adapted to wet, but not flooded soils; often near lakes and marshes; moderately tolerant of salt. Texas distribution: Areas 1, 2, 6

Paspalum notatum
bahiagrass
(inflorescence, Gould and Box, 1965)

BAHIAGRASS

Grass Family (Poaceae: Paniceae)

LATIN NAME: *Paspalum notatum* Flugge

LONGEVITY: Perennial

SEASON: Warm

ORIGIN: Introduced

ECONOMIC VALUE: Wildlife - poor   Livestock - fair

This grass has large, scaly rhizomes. The tough leaves are mostly basal. The seedhead typically has two branches, each with two rows of seeds. The seeds are hard, shiny, and hairless.

FLORAL CHARACTERISTICS:

Inflorescence: panicle, typically of 2 racemose branches; branches 4-15 cm (1 1/2-6 in) long, paired at culm apex, a third branch occasionally present; spikelets occur closely imbricate in two rows along one side of branch

Spikelets: ovate, glabrous, shiny, 2.8-3.5 mm (about 1/8 in) long; 2 florets, lowermost sterile; upper floret perfect, indurate with lemma clasping the palea, straw-colored

Awns: glume, lemmas, and paleas awnless

Glumes: first glume absent, second glume nearly as long as spikelet

VEGETATIVE CHARACTERISTICS:

Culms: 30-75 cm (12-30 in) tall, base decumbent; from thick rhizomes

Leaves: blades glabrous, to 30 cm (12 in) long, about 12 mm (1/2 in) wide, flat, involute or folded

Ligules: dense ring of short hairs, 0.3-0.5 mm (less than 1/64 in) long

GROWTH CHARACTERISTICS:

good salinity tolerance, poor cold tolerance, fair drought tolerance, becomes rank with maturity; reproduces by seeds, tillers, and rhizomes

HABITAT:

adapted to pasture seedings on a wide range of soils, sand to clay. Texas distribution: Areas 1-4

Paspalum plicatulum
brownseed paspalum
(Gould and Box, 1965)

BROWNSEED PASPALUM

Grass Family (Poaceae: Paniceae)

LATIN NAME: *Paspalum plicatulum* Michx.

LONGEVITY: Perennial

SEASON: Warm

ORIGIN: Native

ECONOMIC VALUE: Wildlife - fair Livestock - fair

Known simply as "brownseed", the seeds of this grass turn from gray-green to brown at maturity. The seedhead usually has more branches than dallisgrass. The hairless seeds appear to be in two rows along the branches. The leaf blades are narrower than those of dallisgrass, often are folded near the base and flattening toward the tip.

FLORAL CHARACTERISTICS:

Inflorescence: panicle of 3 to 7 racemose spicate branches each 5-8 cm long; spikelets in 2 rows, paired, on unequal length pedicels on either side of the wavy, flattened branch

Spikelets: 2.4-2.8 mm (3/32-1/8 in) long, round in longitudinal section, flattened on one side in cross section, gray-green turning dark brown at maturity; 2 florets; lemma of upper floret fertile, dark brown, shiny

Awns: glume, lemmas, and paleas awnless

Glumes: first glume missing, second glume glabrous or minutely pubescent

VEGETATIVE CHARACTERISTICS:

Culms: 40-90 cm (16-35 in) tall, from small to large clumps, firm, occasionally with short rhizomes

Leaves: sheath compressed, smooth and paperlike; blades folded, stiff, 25-50 cm (10-20 in) long, hairy near base

Ligules: membranous, 3 mm (1/8 in) long, brown

GROWTH CHARACTERISTICS:

initiates growth in early spring with inflorescences produced from early summer to late fall; reproduces by seeds, tillers, and short rhizomes

HABITAT:

grows well on acid to neutral, poorly drained clay to well drained deep sands; occupies open to shaded sites. Texas distribution: Areas 1-4, 6, 7

Paspalum setaceum
thin paspalum
(Gould and Box, 1965)

THIN PASPALUM

Grass Family (Poaceae: Paniceae)

LATIN NAME: *Paspalum setaceum* Michx.

LONGEVITY: Perennial

SEASON: Warm

ORIGIN: Native

ECONOMIC VALUE: Wildlife - fair   Livestock - fair

This low growing grass has a seedhead with 1-5 branches. The branches have seeds that are round and flattened, seeds occur in two rows along one side in the seedhead branch. Some variations have a fringed leaf blade and hairy sheaths.

FLORAL CHARACTERISTICS:

Inflorescence: spicate raceme or panicle of 2-5 racemose branches, branches 4-16 cm (1 1/2-6 1/4 in) long; axillary inflorescences in leaf sheaths

Spikelets: glabrous to pubescent, elliptic to round, 1.4-2.6 mm (1/32-1/8 in) long; 2 florets

Awns: glume, lemmas, and paleas awnless

Glumes: first glume absent, second glume as long as spikelet

VEGETATIVE CHARACTERISTICS:

Culms: tufted, 30-75 cm (12-30 in) tall from short rhizomes

Leaves: blades flat, soft, 2-20 mm (1/16-3/4 in) wide, glabrous to pubescent, yellow green to dark green

Ligules: membranous, 0.5-1.5 mm (less than 1/16 in) long

GROWTH CHARACTERISTICS:

initiates growth in mid-spring, flowers May to October; tolerant of partial shade; reproduces by seeds, tillers, and rhizomes

HABITAT:

adapted to sandy and loamy soils, on wooded sites, pastures and ditches. Texas distribution: Areas 1-10

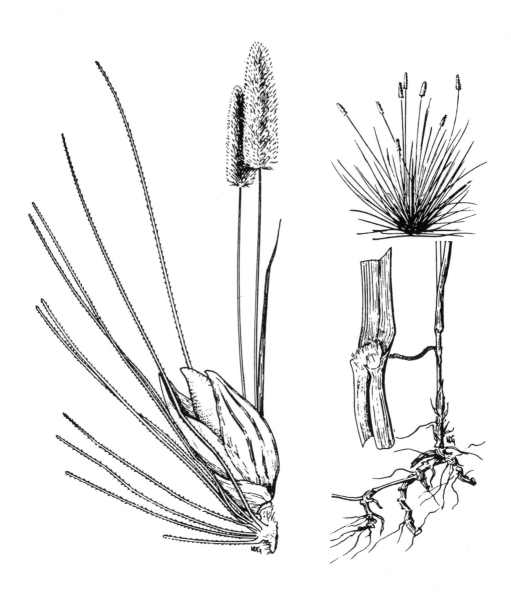

Setaria geniculata
knotroot bristlegrass
(Leithead, 1971)

KNOTROOT BRISTLEGRASS

Grass Family (Poaceae: Paniceae)

LATIN NAME: *Setaria geniculata* (Lam.) Beauv.

LONGEVITY: Perennial

SEASON: Warm

ORIGIN: Native

ECONOMIC VALUE: Wildlife - fair   Livestock - fair

The stems arise from bent, knotty rhizomes, hence the common name. Blades and stems are often purplish. The bristly seedhead commonly matures to a yellow color. Many bristles are below each seed. Leaf blades are usually flat.

FLORAL CHARACTERISTICS:

Inflorescence: panicle, 3-8 cm (1 1/4-3 1/8 in) long, contracted, densely flowered, cylindrical, central axis puberulent; 4-12 bristles below each spikelet, antrorosely scabrous, yellow to tawny at maturity, green or purple in color, 5-10 mm (3/16-3/8 in) long

Spikelets: elliptic, 2.5-3 mm (about 1/8 in) long, turgid, 2 florets; lower lemma texture leaf-like; upper lemma indurate, rugose, acute

Awns: glumes, lemmas, and paleas awnless

Glumes: unequal; first glume one-third spikelet length; second glume two-thirds to three-fourths the spikelet length

VEGETATIVE CHARACTERISTICS:

Culms: tufted, 40-90 cm (16-35 in) tall, nodes glabrous, from a knotty rhizomatous base; rhizomes short

Leaves: glabrous, sheaths keeled; blades flat, 5-30 cm (2-12 in) long, 2-7 mm (1/16-1/4 in) wide

Ligules: ciliate membrane, 0.4-1 mm (less than 1/32 in) long

GROWTH CHARACTERISTICS:

flowers throughout the year with adequate temperature and moisture; reproduces by seeds, tillers, and rhizomes

HABITAT:

moist habitats, ditches, low areas. Texas distribution: Areas 1-10

Texas Range Plants

Setaria leucopila
plains bristlegrass
(Gould and Box, 1965)

PLAINS BRISTLEGRASS

Grass Family (Poaceae: Paniceae)

LATIN NAME:	*Setaria leucopila* (Scribn. & Merr.) Schum.
LONGEVITY:	Perennial
SEASON:	Warm
ORIGIN:	Native
ECONOMIC VALUE:	Wildlife - fair Livestock - good

This bristlegrass has only one bristle below each seed, unlike knotroot bristlegrass which has many bristles. The stems branch at the base and the nodes. Hairs are located just below the stem nodes. Leaf blades are often folded and rough.

FLORAL CHARACTERISTICS:

Inflorescence: panicle, 5-20 cm (2-8 in) long, 6-14 mm (1/4-9/16 in) wide, contracted, cylindrical, densely flowered

Spikelets: 2 florets; spikelet 2-3 mm (1/16-1/8 in) long, subtended by a single bristle; upper lemma rugose, indurate

Awns: glumes, lemmas, and paleas awnless

Glumes: unequal; first glume one-third to one-half the spikelet length

VEGETATIVE CHARACTERISTICS:

Culms: erect or geniculate, 10-100 cm (4-39 in) tall, tufted, hairy below the nodes; branched at the base at lower nodes

Leaves: basal and cauline; sheaths keeled, villous on the upper margins; blades flat or folded, 8-35 cm (3 1/8-14 in) long, 2-10 mm (1/16-3/8 in) wide, glabrous to scabrous

Ligules: ciliate membrane, 1-2 mm (1/32-1/16 in) long, apex rounded

GROWTH CHARACTERISTICS:

starts growth in April to May, may flower more than one time per year depending on available moisture; reproduces by seeds and tillers

HABITAT:

mostly on sandy to sandy loam soils; dry grassland or shrublands. Texas distribution: Areas 2, 5-10

Pappophorum bicolor
pink pappusgrass
(Gould and Box, 1965)

PINK PAPPUSGRASS

Grass Family (Poaceae: Pappophoreae)

LATIN NAME: *Pappophorum bicolor* Fourn.

LONGEVITY: Perennial

SEASON: Warm

ORIGIN: Native

ECONOMIC VALUE: Wildlife - poor   Livestock - fair

Frequently found on sandy or gravelly soils, the seedhead of this bunchgrass is tinged with pink or purple at maturity. The seeds look like small pineapples because of the many bristly awns. The leaves are distinctly heavily veined and the stem nodes are dark in color.

FLORAL CHARACTERISTICS:

Inflorescence: panicle, 10-20 cm (4-8 in) long, contracted, pink or purple tinged at maturity; branches erect to spreading

Spikelets: short pediceled, spikelets 6-8 mm (1/4-5/16 in) long; 3-6 florets, lower 2-3 perfect, upper 2 reduced; lemma 2.5-5 mm (3/32-3/16 in) long, 11-15-nerved, nerves extending into irregular length awns

Awns: glumes awnless; lemmas 11-15 awned; paleas awnless

Glumes: broad, glabrous, acute, mucronate at apex, 3-4 mm (1/8-5/32 in) long

VEGETATIVE CHARACTERISTICS:

Culms: stiffly erect, 30-40 cm (12-16 in) tall, glabrous

Leaves: glabrous; sheaths with hairs near the collar; blades flat or involute, 10-20 cm (4-8 in) long, 2-5 mm (1/16-3/16 in) wide

Ligules: ring of short hairs, 1-4 mm (1/32-5/32 in) long

GROWTH CHARACTERISTICS:

flowers from April to November; reproduces from seeds and tillers

HABITAT:

grassy plains and moist right-of-ways. Texas distribution: Areas 2, 6-8, 10

Bromus unioloides
rescuegrass
(Gould and Box, 1965)

RESCUEGRASS

Grass Family (Poaceae: Poeae)

LATIN NAME: *Bromus unioloides* (Willd.) H.B.K.

LONGEVITY: Annual

SEASON: Cool

ORIGIN: Introduced

ECONOMIC VALUE: Wildlife - fair   Livestock - good

This weedy midgrass is often the first green grass on many sites. The plant earned its common name for coming to the stockman's rescue following drought or winter. The margins of the leaf sheaths are fused. The seedheads droop and the seed bearing structures are strongly flattened.

FLORAL CHARACTERISTICS:

Inflorescence: panicle, 5-30 cm (2-12 in) long, open, drooping

Spikelets: large, 2-3 cm (3/4-1 1/4 in) long, flattened, 6-12 florets; lemmas 7-11-nerved, laterally flattened, strongly keeled, glabrous

Awns: glumes awnless, lemmas awnless to a mucro 3 mm (1/8 in) long

Glumes: unequal; first glume 5-7 nerved; second glume 7-9 nerved; shorter than first floret

VEGETATIVE CHARACTERISTICS:

Culms: erect to ascending, 40-80 cm (16-31 in) tall, tufted

Leaves: basal and cauline; sheaths glabrous to puberulent, margins fused; blades 5-8 mm (3/16-5/16 in) wide, glabrous to puberulent

Ligules: membranous; well-developed; 2-3 mm (1/16-1/8 in) long, lacerate

GROWTH CHARACTERISTICS:

starts growth in late winter, flowers in March or April; reproduces by seeds

HABITAT:

weed of disturbed sites. Texas distribution: Areas 1-10

Festuca arundinacea
tall fescue
(Hitchcock, 1951)

TALL FESCUE

Grass Family (Poaceae: Poeae)

LATIN NAME: *Festuca arundinacea* Schreb.

LONGEVITY: Perennial

SEASON: Cool

ORIGIN: Introduced

ECONOMIC VALUE: Wildlife - fair   Livestock - good

This grass has tall, erect stems coming from a tuft of mostly basal leaves. The leaves are usually flat and covered with minute bristly hairs on the upper surface. There are 5 to 8 seeds in each cluster and the outer surface of each seed is nerved.

FLORAL CHARACTERISTICS:

Inflorescence: panicle, 10-30 cm (4-12 in) long, erect to nodding, contracted, occasionally lower branches spreading, pedicels short

Spikelets: appressed, 10-16 mm (3/8-5/8 in) long; 5-8 florets; lemmas 6-9 mm (1/4-11/32 in) long, 5-nerved

Awns: glumes awnless; lemmas awnless or awned to 4 mm (5/32 in) long

Glumes: lanceolate, 4-7 mm (5/32-1/4 in) long, second glume slightly longer than the first

VEGETATIVE CHARACTERISTICS:

Culms: erect, 50-120 cm (20-59 in) tall, tufted

Leaves: basal and cauline; sheaths smooth to scabrous, rounded on the back; blades flat or folded, 4-13 mm (5/32-1/2 in) wide, margins scabrous

Ligules: ciliate membrane, to 2 mm (1/16 in) long

GROWTH CHARACTERISTICS:

flowers April to June, may remain green into summer with adequate moisture; reproduces by seeds and tillers

HABITAT:

mostly in seeded pastures or near one. Texas distribution: Areas 3-5, 7-9

Lolium perenne
ryegrass
(Hitchcock, 1951)

RYEGRASS

Grass Family (Poaceae: Poeae)

LATIN NAME: *Lolium perenne* L.

LONGEVITY: Annual

SEASON: Cool

ORIGIN: Introduced

ECONOMIC VALUE: Wildlife - fair   Livestock - fair

This introduced annual grass has adapted to a wide variety of sites throughout Texas. The seedhead does not branch and the groups of seeds are laid edgewise, closely arranged on the main stem which is slightly zig-zag. The leaves are smooth and shiny. There are prominent clasping auricles at the top of each leaf sheath. May contain estrogenic compounds associated with poor reproduction in game birds.

FLORAL CHARACTERISTICS:

Inflorescence: spike, 10-25 cm (4-10 in) long, 10-25 spikelets; spikelets edgewise to rachis

Spikelets: single at each node, laterally flattened; 5-12 florets

Awns: glumes awnless; lemmas awnless to an awn 8 mm (5/16 in) long

Glumes: first glume absent, except on terminal spikelet; second glume 5-10 mm (3/16-3/8 in) long, one-third to two-thirds the length of the spikelet

VEGETATIVE CHARACTERISTICS:

Culms: erect, 25-80 cm (10-31 in) tall, glabrous, thick and succulent

Leaves: basal and cauline; sheaths thin, margins hyaline; auricles membranous; blades 3-12 mm (1/8-1/2 in) wide

Ligules: membranous, 1-2 mm (1/32-1/16 in) long, apex truncate

GROWTH CHARACTERISTICS:

initiates growth in January or February, flowers March to June; reproduces by seeds

HABITAT:

cultivated pasture grass or weed; planted along roadsides. Texas distribution: Areas 1-9

Poa arachnifera
Texas bluegrass

TEXAS BLUEGRASS

Grass Family (Poaceae: Poeae)

LATIN NAME: *Poa arachnifera* Torr.

LONGEVITY: Perennial

SEASON: Cool

ORIGIN: Native

ECONOMIC VALUE: Wildlife - fair   Livestock - good

An important rhizomatous grass that grows in the cool season. Leaf blades are folded and resemble the keel of a boat at the apex. The seeds are on a narrow congested seedhead. Male and female plants grow separately. Male seedheads appear smooth while female seedheads have hairs that resemble cobwebs hence the Latin name "arachnifera".

FLORAL CHARACTERISTICS:

Inflorescence: panicle, 5-14 cm (2-5 1/2 in) long, contracted to lobed, branches with spikelets to near the base or without spikelets on the lower half of the branches

Spikelets: unisexual; 3-9 florets; pistillate spikelets densely pubescent, 5-6 mm (3/16-1/4 in) long, lemmas 5-nerved with kinky hairs near the base; staminate spikelets not conspicuously hairy, 3-5 mm (1/8-1/4 in) long

Awns: glumes, lemmas, and paleas awnless

Glumes: unequal, apex acute to acuminate, shorter than the first floret; second glume longer than the first

VEGETATIVE CHARACTERISTICS:

Culms: erect, 30-60 cm (12-24 in) tall, tufted; slender rhizomes present

Leaves: glabrous; blades usually flat, 2-4 mm (1/16-5/32 in) wide, elongate

Ligules: membranous, about 0.5 mm (less than 1/32 in) long, acute

GROWTH CHARACTERISTICS:

plant dioecious; flowers from April to June; reproduces from seeds and rhizomes; reportedly a highly valuable forage for livestock in the cool season

HABITAT:

clay or clay loam soils of grasslands, margins of woods; not in disturbed habitats. Texas distribution: Areas 1-5, 7, 8

Stipa leucotricha
Texas wintergrass
(inflorescence and spikelet, Gould and Box, 1965)
(base and cleistogamous spikelet, Leithead, 1971)

TEXAS WINTERGRASS

Grass Family (Poaceae: Stipeae)

LATIN NAME: *Stipa leucotricha* Trin. & Rupr.

LONGEVITY: Perennial

SEASON: Cool

ORIGIN: Native

ECONOMIC VALUE: Wildlife - fair   Livestock - fair

The common name of this grass refers to the fact that it grows throughout the winter. The leaves are dark green, very erect, and covered with short, stiff hairs. The sharp based seeds have long, bent and twisted awns which lend the grass the common name "speargrass". Papery white bracts (glumes) resembling oats remain after the seed falls. The plant commonly has seeds hidden in the basal leaf sheaths.

FLORAL CHARACTERISTICS:

Inflorescence: panicle, 6-25 cm (2 3/8-10 in) long, 5-12 cm (2-4 3/4 in) wide, branches flexuous

Spikelets: 1 floret; lemma 9-12 mm (11/32-1/2 in) long, oblong light brown; lemma apex has a white crown with stiff hairs 0.5-1 mm (1/32 in or less) long; cleistogamous spikelets produced in many basal sheaths

Awns: glumes awnless; lemma awn, 4-10 cm (1 1/2-4 in) once or twice geniculate, twisted, stout

Glumes: longer than the lemma, nearly equal, 12-18 mm (1/2-11/16 in) long, glabrous

VEGETATIVE CHARACTERISTICS:

Culms: caespitose, 30-90 cm (12-35 in) tall, base spreading, nodes pubescent

Leaves: sheaths pubescent to glabrous; collar with long hairs at the margins; blades flat, 5-40 cm (2-16 in) long, 1-5 mm (1/32-3/16 in) wide, usually with short stiff hairs on both surfaces

Ligules: membranous, 0.2-1 mm (1/32 in or less) long, apex truncate

GROWTH CHARACTERISTICS:

starts growth in late fall, continues slow growth through winter and then grows and matures rapidly in the spring; reproduces from seeds, cleistogamous spikelets, and tillers

HABITAT:

dry prairies, sandy or clayey soils; moderately disturbed sites, especially on heavily grazed sites. Texas distribution: Areas 1-10

Elymus canadensis
Canada wildrye
(Hitchcock, 1951)

CANADA WILDRYE

Grass Family (Poaceae: Triticeae)

LATIN NAME: *Elymus canadensis* L.

LONGEVITY: Perennial

SEASON: Cool

ORIGIN: Native

ECONOMIC VALUE: Wildlife - fair   Livestock - good

This cool season grass is most often dark green in color and found on sites with extra moisture available. The leaf blades are wide, with clasping, conspicuous auricles. The glumes at the base of the seed form a "V". The seedhead is drooping at maturity.

FLORAL CHARACTERISTICS:

Inflorescence: spike, 7-23 cm (2 3/4-9 in) long, usually nodding, thick, with 2-4 spikelets per node

Spikelets: 2-6 florets; lemmas 8-10 mm (5/16-3/8 in) long, hispid or scabrous

Awns: glumes with awn 1-3 mm (3/8-1 1/4 in) long; lemma awn 15-40 mm (9/16-1 1/2 in) long, curving outward from the rachis at maturity

Glumes: narrow, nearly equal, tapering to an awn

VEGETATIVE CHARACTERISTICS:

Culms: decumbent at the base, 1-1.5 m (39-59 in) tall, tufted

Leaves: sheaths glabrous; auricles well-developed, clasping; blades 5-45 cm (2-18 in) long, 7-20 mm (1/4-3/4 in) wide, midrib prominent beneath

Ligules: membranous, 0.5-1 mm (1/32 in or less) long, truncate, apex minutely ciliate

GROWTH CHARACTERISTICS:

initiates growth in the fall and grows slowly through the winter, matures in late spring to early summer; reproduces by seeds and tillers

HABITAT:

prairies, especially moist woods and roadsides. Texas distribution: Areas 1-5, 7-10

Elymus virginicus
Virginia wildrye
(Leithead, 1971)

VIRGINIA WILDRYE

Grass Family (Poaceae: Triticeae)

LATIN NAME: *Elymus virginicus* L.

LONGEVITY: Perennial

SEASON: Cool

ORIGIN: Native

ECONOMIC VALUE: Wildlife - fair   Livestock - good

Unlike Canada wildrye, this grass tolerates slightly drier habitats, and is found in the more western locations in Texas. The leaf blades are not as wide as those of Canada wildrye. Clasping auricles are present at the sheath apex. The glumes are bowed at the base forming a "U" shape. The seedhead remains erect.

FLORAL CHARACTERISTICS:

Inflorescence: spike, 8-16 cm (3 1/8-6 1/4 in) long, stiff, erect; spikelets 2-3 per node

Spikelets: 2 or more florets, uppermost floret reduced

Awns: glumes awned; lemma awn 5-20 mm (3/16-3/4 in) long, straight to slightly curved

Glumes: nearly equal, strongly bowed out at base, strongly nerved, base yellow

VEGETATIVE CHARACTERISTICS:

Culms: tufted, 40-80 cm (16-31 in) tall, erect or decumbent, green to glabrous

Leaves: cauline and basal; sheaths glabrous; auricles well-developed, clasping; blades 5-12 mm (3/16-1/2 in) wide, flat, glabrous

Ligules: membranous, to 0.5 mm (less than 1/32 in) long, apex truncate

GROWTH CHARACTERISTICS:

flowers April to June; reproduces by seeds and tillers

HABITAT:

shaded soils from sands to clays, found in higher precipitation or runoff areas. Texas distribution: Areas 1-8

Elytrigia smithii
western wheatgrass
(Judd, 1962)

WESTERN WHEATGRASS

Grass Family (Poaceae: Triticeae)

LATIN NAME: *Elytrigia smithii* (Rydb.) Nevski
(*Agropyron smithii* Rydb.)

LONGEVITY: Perennial

SEASON: Cool

ORIGIN: Native

ECONOMIC VALUE: Wildlife - fair Livestock - good

This strongly rhizomatous grass is stiffly erect. The leaf blades are rough textured. The seeds on the spike-type seedhead overlap the next by one-half their length. In the field, western wheatgrass is usually a characteristic blue-green color.

FLORAL CHARACTERISTICS:

Inflorescence: spike, 6-16 cm (2 3/8-6 1/4 in) long; spikelets overlap the next spikelet by one-half their length; occasionally 2 spikelets per node

Spikelets: 5-12 florets; spikelet 1.5-2/6 cm (1/2-1 in) long, glaucous; lemmas several-nerved, glabrous to pubescent

Awns: glumes awnless to awn-tipped; lemmas awnless to awn-tipped

Glumes: asymmetrical, slightly curved, faintly nerved, rigid

VEGETATIVE CHARACTERISTICS:

Culms: erect, 35-85 cm (14-33 in) tall, small tufts from a rhizomatous base, glaucous

Leaves: sheaths glabrous to scabrous, auricles present or absent, when present 1-2 mm (1/32-1/16 in) long; blades stiffly ascending, 10-20 cm (4-8 in) long, 2-7 mm (1/16-1/4 in) wide, strongly ribbed, involute upon drying, glaucous

Ligules: membranous, about 1 mm (1/32 in) long, apex truncate or minutely ciliate

GROWTH CHARACTERISTICS:

growth starts when temperatures reach 53°F (12°C), usually dormant in the Texas summers; reproduces from seeds, tillers, and rhizomes

HABITAT:

most common on low, moist flats or flood plains, less frequent on dry sites. Texas distribution: Areas 4, 7-10

Hordeum pusillum
little barley
(Gould and Box, 1965)

LITTLE BARLEY

Grass Family (Poaceae: Triticeae)

LATIN NAME: *Hordeum pusillum* Nutt.

LONGEVITY: Annual

SEASON: Cool

ORIGIN: Native

ECONOMIC VALUE: Wildlife - poor   Livestock - poor

This annual grass greens up very early and matures to a straw yellow color quickly. Its size may vary greatly depending upon moisture available for growth. The seedhead has many fine awns. The leaves are short, flat and very erect.

FLORAL CHARACTERISTICS:

Inflorescence: spicate raceme, 2-8 cm (3/4-3 1/8 in) long, erect, narrow; spikelets 3 per node, 1 sessile and fertile, 2 lateral spikelets pedicellate and sterile

Spikelets: 1 floret; lemma of sessile spikelet 2-3 times the length of the lateral spikelet lemma

Awns: glumes reduced to awns, 7-15 mm (1/4-9/16 in) long; lemma awn of sessile spikelet 2-7 mm (1/16-1/4 in) long

Glumes: slightly dilated above the base, scabrous

VEGETATIVE CHARACTERISTICS:

Culms: tufted, 10-40 cm (4-16 in) tall, base geniculate

Leaves: sheaths round, glabrous, usually with auricles; blades flat, 1-12 cm (3/8-4 3/4 in) long, 2-5 mm (1/16-3/16 in) wide, ascending

Ligules: membranous, 0.4-0.7 mm (less than 1/32 in) long, apex erose

GROWTH CHARACTERISTICS:

germinates in early spring, matures by late spring; reproduces by seeds

HABITAT:

waste places, disturbed sites; especially alkaline areas. Texas distribution: Areas 1-10

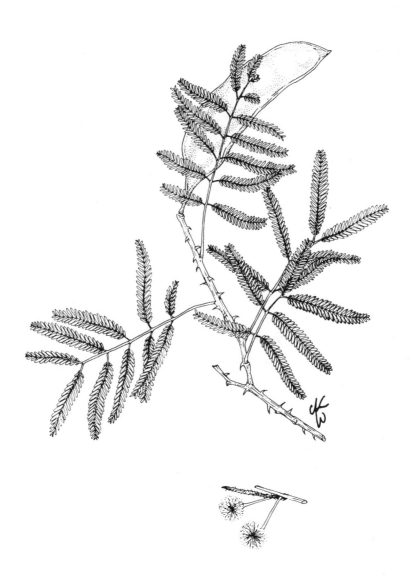

Acacia berlandieri
guajillo

GUAJILLO

Legume Family (Fabaceae)

LATIN NAME: *Acacia berlandieri* Benth.

LONGEVITY: Perennial

SEASON: Warm

ORIGIN: Native

ECONOMIC VALUE: Wildlife - fair   Livestock - fair (poisonous)

Guajillo is named for Luis Berlandier, a Belgian botanist who worked along the U.S. - Mexican border in the early 1800's. Guajillo, a famous honey plant, is also widely used ornamentally. It may be propagated by seeds or transplanting seedlings.

GROWTH CHARACTERISTICS:

shrub, 1.3-5 m (3-9 ft) tall, branched at base; flowers November to March, fruits mature by summer; reproduces by seeds

DISTINGUISHING CHARACTERISTICS:

Leaves: compound, bipinnate, deciduous; leaflets 4 mm (5/32 in) long, narrow, fern-like in appearance, 30-50 pairs, pubescent to glabrous

Flowers: white to yellow in globose heads, heads about 1 cm (3/8 in) in diameter; corolla 5-parted, pubescent; stamens exserted, numerous

Fruit: legume, 8-16 cm (3 1/8-6 1/4 in) long, 15-25 mm (9/16-1 in) wide, flat, margins thickened, velvety tomentose

Other: stem internodes usually armed with prickles 1-3 mm (1/32-1/8 in) long, prickles recurved

LIVESTOCK LOSSES:

may cause hydrocyanic acid poisoning in livestock

HABITAT:

limestone and caliche hills and sandy soil. Texas distribution: Areas 2, 6, 7

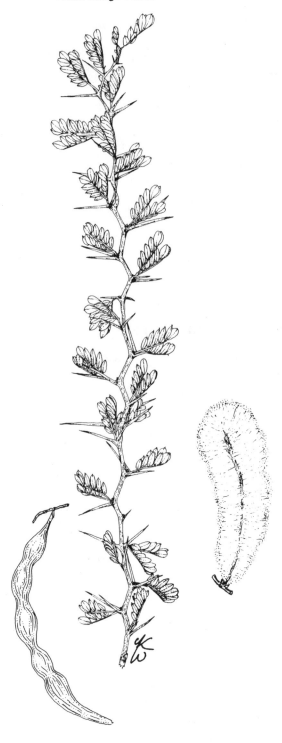

Acacia rigidula
blackbrush

BLACKBRUSH

Legume Family (Fabaceae)

LATIN NAME: *Acacia rigidula* Benth.

LONGEVITY: Perennial

SEASON: Warm

ORIGIN: Native

ECONOMIC VALUE: Wildlife - fair   Livestock - poor

Blackbrush has spines long and sharp enough to cause flat tires. It has not been cultivated as widely as other acacias. Blackbrush can grow in thickets that are virtually impenetrable in west and southwest Texas.

GROWTH CHARACTERISTICS:

shrub, 1-3 m (3-9 ft) tall, much branched from base, thicket forming, flowers April to May; reproduces by seeds

DISTINGUISHING CHARACTERISTICS:

Leaves: compound, bipinnate, deciduous; leaflets in 2-4 pairs, 6-15 mm (1/4-9/16 in) long, dark green, glabrous, oblique, oblong, base asymmetrical

Flowers: in axillary spikes, fragrant; calyx 4-5-parted; corolla white to yellow, 4-5 petals; stamens exserted

Fruit: legume, 6-8 cm (2 3/8-3 1/8 in) long, nearly round in cross-section, slightly constricted between seeds, apex acuminate

LIVESTOCK LOSSES:

spines may cause injury

HABITAT:

sandy or limestone areas, may provide valuable erosion control. Texas distribution: Areas 2, 6, 7, 10

Acacia smallii
huisache

HUISACHE

Legume Family (Fabaceae)

LATIN NAME: *Acacia smallii* Isely
                        (*Acacia farnesiana* (L.) Willd.)

LONGEVITY: Perennial

SEASON: Warm

ORIGIN: Native

ECONOMIC VALUE: Wildlife - poor   Livestock - poor

"Sweet acacia", a prized honey plant, is commonly cultivated as an ornamental in tropical countries. Glue from the pods has been used to mend pottery. Fragrant oils extracted from the plant are used to make perfumes. Early peoples reportedly use the fruits, bark, and roots for various medicinal purposes.

GROWTH CHARACTERISTICS:

shrub or small tree, 2-10 m (6-30 ft) tall, much branched from the base; flowers in the early spring; reproduces by seeds

DISTINGUISHING CHARACTERISTICS:

Leaves: compound, bipinnate, deciduous; leaflets 3-5 mm (1/8-3/16 in) long, 10-25 pair, linear, gray-green, base asymetrical

Flowers: in globose clusters, yellow; heads 1 cm (3/8 in) in diameter, fragrant; corolla 5 parted; stamens numerous, yellow, exserted

Fruit: legume, 2-8 cm (3/4-3 1/8 in) long, tapered at both ends, circular in cross-section; seeds in two rows, black

Other: stipular spines paired, straight, white, rigid

LIVESTOCK LOSSES:

mechanical injury may occur from tissue contact with spines

HABITAT:

dry, sandy soils, moist sand and clay, disturbed pastures. Texas distribution: Areas 2-4, 6, 7

Astragalus mollissimus
wooly loco
(Stubbendieck et al., 1982)

WOOLY LOCO

Legume Family (Fabaceae)

LATIN NAME:	*Astragalus mollissimus* Torr.
LONGEVITY:	Perennial
SEASON:	Cool
ORIGIN:	Native
ECONOMIC VALUE:	Wildlife - poor Livestock - poor (poisonous)

The genus Astragalus *is very large with more than 1500 members. The plant is also known as "crazy loco", "Texas loco", and "purple locoweed". It is thought to be one of the first recognized members of the genus. Wooly loco is a relatively short-lived perennial.*

GROWTH CHARACTERISTICS:

forb, 10-38 cm (4-16 in) tall, initiates growth in March, fruits mature by June; reproduces by seeds

DISTINGUISHING CHARACTERISTICS:

Leaves: compound, odd-pinnate; leaflets 11-33, 5-25 mm (3/16-1 in) long, 2-15 mm (1/16-9/16 in) wide, ovate, apex rounded, villous to tomentose; stipules free from base of petiole

Flowers: in a raceme; calyx tube 7-9 mm (1/4-3/8 in) long, silky; corolla purple to pink, 18 mm (11/16 in) long, keel petal rounded, papilionaceous

Fruit: legume, 9-25 mm (3/8-1 in) long, linear-oblong, apex acuminate

Other: stems and leaves densely canescent

LIVESTOCK LOSSES:

loco disease in horses, cattle, sheep, and goats caused by lococine; selenium poisoning can occur when plants grow in selenium bearing soils

HABITAT:

plains and prairies. Texas distribution: Areas 8-10

Astragalus nuttallianus var. *nuttallianus*
nuttall milkvetch

NUTTALL MILKVETCH

Legume Family (Fabaceae)

LATIN NAME:	*Astragalus nuttallianus* A. DC. var. *nuttallianus*
LONGEVITY:	Annual
SEASON:	Cool
ORIGIN:	Native
ECONOMIC VALUE:	Wildlife - poor Livestock - fair (poisonous)

Because of the nature of the poison reaction of Nuttall milkvetch, it also has earned the common names "locoweed" and "crazyweed". Poisoning may occur on soils with high selenium content as the plants accumulate selenium in addition to "lococine". Nuttall milkvetch is not a true vetch. True members of the vetch genus family (<u>Vicia</u> spp.) are characterized by having tendrils.

GROWTH CHARACTERISTICS:

forb, usually less than 25 cm (10 in) long, stems slender, glabrous to glabrate, green to silvery canescent; reproduces by seeds

DISTINGUISHING CHARACTERISTICS:

Leaves: alternate, pinnately compound, petioled, 1-6 cm (3/8-2 3/8 in) long; stipules free, well-developed bracts; leaflets 7-21, odd pinnate, linear to elliptical, 2-10 mm (1/16-3/8 in) long, apex truncate to emarginate

Flowers: in axillary racemes; papilionaceous; calyx 5-parted; corolla whitish to purplish to purple, 4-10 mm (5/32-3/8 in) long

Fruit: legume, 16-25 mm (5/8-1 in) long, linear, curved, nearly terete; seeds 2-3 mm (1/16-1/8 in) long, shiny, yellow with purple spots

Other: life span 3-4 months

LIVESTOCK LOSSES:

toxic to cattle, sheep, and goats except when in soils of igneous origins; symptoms include loss of weight, incoordination of hind legs and paralysis; plant is susceptible to herbicides

HABITAT:

rocky and sandy prairies, desert grassland, roadsides, and savannahs. Texas distribution: Areas 1, 3-8

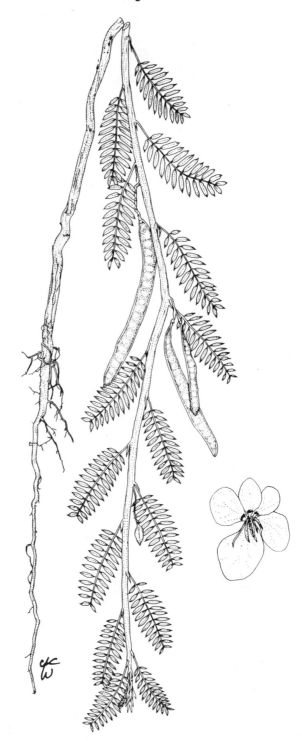

Chamaecrista fasciculata
showy partridgepea

SHOWY PARTRIDGEPEA

Legume Family (Fabaceae)

LATIN NAME:	*Chamaecrista fasciculata* (Michx.) Greene (*Cassia fasciculata* Michx.)
LONGEVITY:	Annual
SEASON:	Warm
ORIGIN:	Native
ECONOMIC VALUE:	Wildlife - poor Livestock - fair

Showy partridgepea is often covered with ants trailing up and down the stem where they are feeding on nectar from small glands at the base of the leaves. The adult common sulfur butterfly lays her eggs on the leaves of the plant and the larvae feed upon the leaves. The seeds of showy partridgepea are valuable food for many birds, both game and songbird species.

GROWTH CHARACTERISTICS:

forb, 20-120 cm (8-47 in) tall; stems erect, glabrous at maturity; reproduces by seeds

DISTINGUISHING CHARACTERISTICS:

Leaves: alternate, pinnately compound; stipules 5-10 mm (3/16-3/8 in) long, linear; leaflets 8-14 pair, 1-2 cm (3/8-3/4 in) long, 2-4 mm (1/16-5/32 in) wide, linear, glabrous

Flowers: axillary, 2-7 per raceme; sepals 8-16 mm (5/16-5/8 in) long, lanceolate, apex acuminate; petals 5, obovate, 9-15 mm (11/32-9/16 in) long, the two lower petals shorter, yellow; stamens 10, yellow, anthers curved

Fruit: legume, 5-8 cm (2-3 1/8 in) long, 3-6 mm (1/8-1/4 in) wide, flattened, linear; seeds 10-20, dark brown

Other: petiole with small glands below the lowest leaflets

LIVESTOCK LOSSES:

HABITAT:

open fields, disturbed sites, sandy soils throughout much of the State. Texas distribution: Areas 1-9

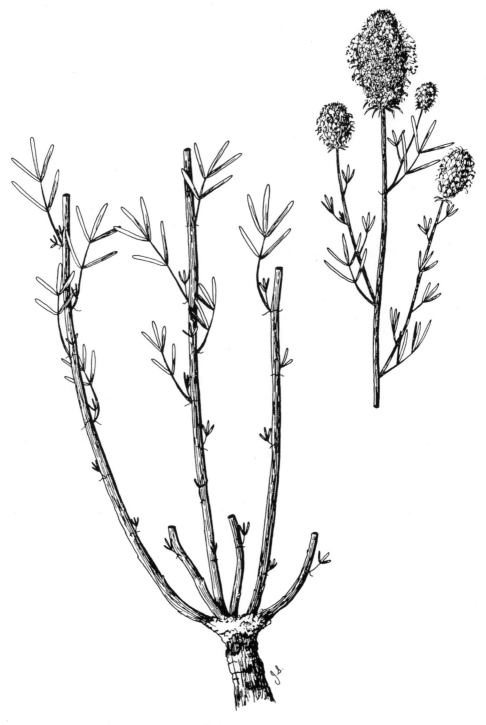

Dalea purpurea
purple prairieclover
(Wasser, 1982)

PURPLE PRAIRIECLOVER

Legume Family (Fabaceae)

LATIN NAME: *Dalea purpurea* Vent.
                        (*Petalostemum purpureum* (Vent.) Rydb.)

LONGEVITY: Perennial

SEASON: Warm

ORIGIN: Native

ECONOMIC VALUE: Wildlife - good   Livestock - good

Purple prairieclover is a highly nutritious forage. The tender new growth is particularly high in protein, thus making it a valuable wildlife forage.

GROWTH CHARACTERISTICS:

forb, 20-60 cm (8-24 in) tall, erect or ascending; flowers in June to July; reproduces by seeds and rootstock

DISTINGUISHING CHARACTERISTICS:

Leaves: alternate, pinnately compound; leaflets 5, mostly linear, folded, glabrous to villous, glandular-punctate below

Flowers: irregular, in dense oval shaped spikes; spikes 1-5 cm (3/8-2 in) long; calyx 2.5-4 mm long, villous; corolla lavender

Fruit: legume, 2.5-3.5 mm (1/16-1/8 in) long, pubescent

Other: taproot woody

LIVESTOCK LOSSES:

may cause bloat

HABITAT:

prairies, plains, and hills. Texas distribution: Areas 4, 5, 8, 10

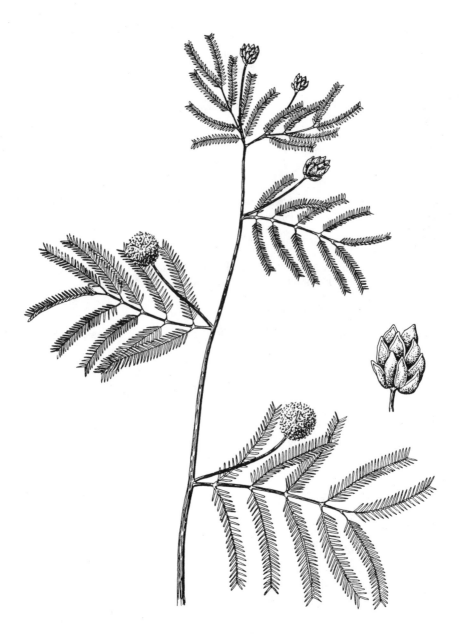

Desmanthus illinoensis
Illinois bundleflower
(Wasser, 1982)

ILLINOIS BUNDLEFLOWER

Legume Family (Fabaceae)

LATIN NAME: *Desmanthus illinoensis* (Michx.) MacM.

LONGEVITY: Perennial

SEASON: Warm

ORIGIN: Native

ECONOMIC VALUE: Wildlife - good   Livestock - good

The common name "bundleflower" is descriptive of the unusual arrangement of seeds in a twisted bundle. Illinois bundleflower is one of the most important native legumes, valued as forage for domestic livestock and wildlife.

GROWTH CHARACTERISTICS:

forb, 60-130 cm (24-51 in) tall; stems angled, glabrous, single or several from a woody crown; reproduces by seeds, rootstocks, and rhizomes

DISTINGUISHING CHARACTERISTICS:

Leaves: alternate; bipinnately compound; stipules bristlelike; pinnae in 6-14 pairs; leaflets 20-30 per pinnae, linear, glabrous to pubescent

Flowers: in globose heads; calyx 5-parted; corolla 5-parted, white, stamens 10

Fruit: legume, flat, spirally twisted, 15-25 mm (1/32-1/16 in) long, 4-5 mm (5/32-3/16 in) wide, seeds 2-6

Other: leaflets sensitive to bright sunlight and touching, when stimulated they fold inward

LIVESTOCK LOSSES:

HABITAT:

tallgrass prairies, savannahs; frequently in clay soils. Texas distribution: Areas 2-5, 7-10

Lathyrus hirsutus
singletary pea

SINGLETARY PEA

Legume Family (Fabaceae)

LATIN NAME: *Lathyrus hirsutus* L.

LONGEVITY: Annual

SEASON: Cool

ORIGIN: Introduced

ECONOMIC VALUE: Wildlife - fair   Livestock - good

This species, native to southern Europe, is widespread and becoming naturalized from Texas to Virginia. Singletary pea is a winter annual planted to supplement forage and add protein to diets of livestock on dry, native rangelands. In some areas the species is used to improve soil because of nitrogen fixing attributes.

GROWTH CHARACTERISTICS:

forb, 20-100 cm (8-39 in) long; stems clambering to climbing, winged; reproduces by seeds

DISTINGUISHING CHARACTERISTICS:

Leaves: alternate, compound, pinnate; stipules linear, entire, hirsute; leaflets 2, linear to oblong, entire, 2-7 cm (3/4-2 3/4 in) long; tendrils well-developed, branched

Flowers: single or in axillary racemes; sepals 5, toothed, 5-7 mm (3/16-1/4 in) long; corolla papilionaceous, white or pink; stamens 10, diadelphous

Fruit: legume, 20-35 mm (3/4-1 3/8 in) long, 4-8 mm (5/32-5/16 in) wide, flattened, hirsute, 4-12 seeded

LIVESTOCK LOSSES:

HABITAT:

escaped from introduced plantings to disturbed sites such as roadsides. Texas distribution: Areas 1, 3, 4

Lupinus subcarnosus
Texas bluebonnet

TEXAS BLUEBONNET

Legume Family (Fabaceae)

LATIN NAME: *Lupinus subcarnosus* Hook.

LONGEVITY: Annual

SEASON: Cool

ORIGIN: Native

ECONOMIC VALUE: Wildlife - poor   Livestock - poor

By law in 1901, <u>Lupinus subcarnatus</u> was named the State Flower of Texas. Because another species, <u>Lupinus texansis</u> was more showy and prolific, the law was modified in 1971 so both species are considered as the State Flower. Propagation of Texas bluebonnet has been aided by the Highway Beautification Program which started during Lyndon Johnson's presidency as the pet project of the First Lady.

GROWTH CHARACTERISTICS:

forb, 15-45 cm (6-18 in) tall; stems branched at base, silky pubescent; reproduces by seeds

DISTINGUISHING CHARACTERISTICS:

Leaves: alternate, palmately compound, petiole twice the length of the longest leaflet; leaflets usually 5, oblanceolate, apex rounded to truncate

Flowers: in racemes, 6-15 cm (2 3/8-6 in) long, several flowered, apex rounded; flowers blue and white, papilionaceous; calyx 5-6 mm (3/16-1/4 in) long, with 4 teeth; corolla 10-13 mm (3/8-1/2 in) long, purplish with age

Fruit: legume, 2-4 cm (3/4-1 1/2 in) long, 8-10 mm (5/16-3/8 in) wide, slightly constricted between the 4-5 seeds; seeds gray, tan, or spotted, about 5 mm (3/16 in) wide

Other: seeds resemble small pieces of rock; spread by humans

LIVESTOCK LOSSES:

HABITAT:

abundant in fine sand to sandy loam or podsol. Texas distribution: Areas 2-6

Medicago polymorpha
bur-clover

BUR-CLOVER

Legume Family (Fabaceae)

LATIN NAME: *Medicago polymorpha* L.

LONGEVITY: Annual

SEASON: Cool

ORIGIN: Introduced

ECONOMIC VALUE: Wildlife - fair   Livestock - good

Bur-clover has naturalized to many parts of Texas, especially where it has been planted as a winter feed source. It is a valuable deer forage, but the burs accumulate in the wool of domestic sheep and the hair of angora goats and can decrease the value of the wool and the hair.

GROWTH CHARACTERISTICS:

forb, 15-55 cm (6-22 in) long; stems prostrate to ascending; flowers in early spring; matures in 6-8 weeks; reproduces by seeds

DISTINGUISHING CHARACTERISTICS:

Leaves: alternate, pinnately compound, trifoliate, petiolate; stipules leaf-like, 6-11 mm (1/4-1/2 in) long, paired; leaflets 1-1.5 cm (3/8-9/16 in) long, cuneate, ovate to obovate, serrate, sometimes with purple or white spots

Flowers: in small clusters of 2-5 flowers; calyx pubescent, 5-parted, about 1 mm (1/32 in) long; corolla yellow, 4-5 mm (5/32-3/16 in) long, papilionaceous

Fruit: legume, spirally coiled 2-5 times; spines 2-3 mm (1/16-1/8 in) long, hooked

Other: stems glabrous to puberulent

LIVESTOCK LOSSES:

excessive use can cause bloat in domestic livestock; wool value decreases when large numbers of burs are present

HABITAT:

disturbed sites, common lawn weed. Texas distribution: Areas 2-7, 10

Texas Range Plants

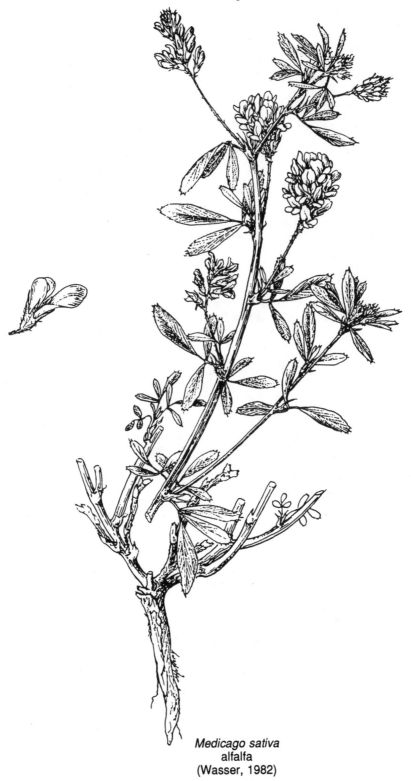

Medicago sativa
alfalfa
(Wasser, 1982)

ALFALFA

Legume Family (Fabaceae)

LATIN NAME: *Medicago sativa* L.

LONGEVITY: Perennial

SEASON: Warm

ORIGIN: Introduced

ECONOMIC VALUE: Wildlife - good   Livestock - good

This nitrogen fixing legume, also known as "lucerne", was introduced from Europe to produce a high quality forage that was high in protein. Alfalfa has been cultivated for 2500 years or more as a hay and to increase nitrogen in the soil.

GROWTH CHARACTERISTICS:

forb, 30-100 cm (12-39 in) tall; stems erect to ascending; reproduces by seeds; generally completes the growth cycle in the early summer

DISTINGUISHING CHARACTERISTICS:

Leaves: alternate, compound, leaflets 3; leaflets 1-3 cm (3/8-1 1/4 in) long, 3-9 mm (1/8-3/8 in) wide, obovate to oblong; stipules 6-18 mm (1/4-11/16 in) long, fused to petiole base

Flowers: in crowded racemes, 1-4 cm (3/8-1 1/2 in) long, 1-2.5 cm (3/8-1 in) wide, with 10-30 flowers; petals 7-13 mm (1/4-1/2 in) long, blue violet, papilionaceous

Fruit: legume, loosely to spirally coiled, coils 4-5 mm (5/32-3/16 in) in diameter, without prickles on the margins

LIVESTOCK LOSSES:

ingested plants can cause bloat from nitrates; acute nitrate poisoning can result in the quick death of many animals; cattle, sheep, goats, and horses are affected

HABITAT:

usually a forage crop but escapes along roadsides and in abandoned fields. Texas distribution: Areas 1-5, 7-10

Melilotus albus
white sweetclover
(Forest Service, 1937)

WHITE SWEETCLOVER

Legume Family (Fabaceae)

LATIN NAME: *Melilotus albus* Lam.

LONGEVITY: Annual (occasionally biennial)

SEASON: Cool

ORIGIN: Introduced

ECONOMIC VALUE: Wildlife - fair   Livestock - good

Like many other legumes, white sweetclover was carried to North America by early European settlers. A group of the plants gives off a strong, sweet perfume. The genus name is derived from the Greek word "meli" meaning honey. The plant is indeed a valuable honey plant as well as a desirable forage and cover crop.

GROWTH CHARACTERISTICS:

forb, 20-160 cm (8-63 in) tall; reproduces by seeds

DISTINGUISHING CHARACTERISTICS:

Leaves: alternate; compound, pinnately trifoliate; stipules fused toward the base; leaflets oblanceolate to obovate, margins minutely serrate

Flowers: in racemes of 35-75 flowers; sepals green; small petals 3-5 mm (1/8-3/16 in) long, white, papilionaceous; stamens 10, diadelphous

Fruit: legume, 1.8-3.4 mm (1/16-1/8 in) long, 1.8-3.4 mm (1/16-1/8 in) wide, globose, nearly indehiscent, 1-seeded, glabrous

LIVESTOCK LOSSES:

dicumarol may poison cattle and sheep; causes internal hemorrhages; treat with hemostatic solution to increase the rate of blood coagulation

HABITAT:

weed of disturbed habitats; planted to help increase soil nitrogen. Texas distribution: Areas 2-10

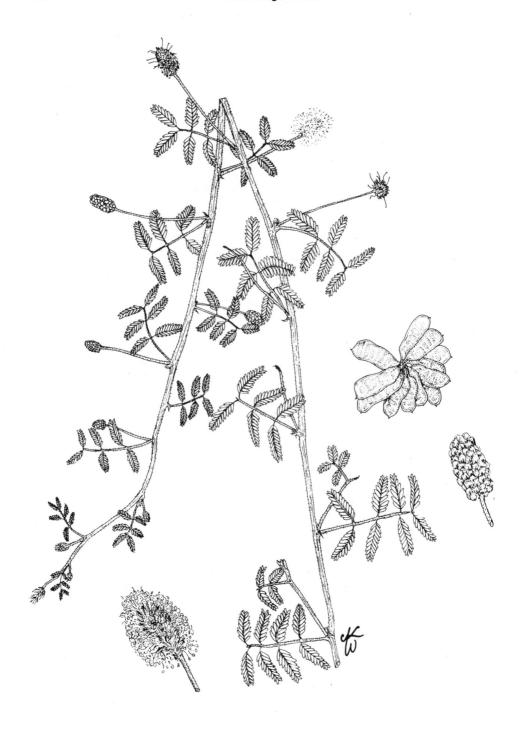

Neptunea lutea
yellow neptunia

YELLOW NEPTUNIA

Legume Family (Fabaceae)

LATIN NAME: *Neptunea lutea* (Leavenw.) Benth.

LONGEVITY: Perennial

SEASON: Warm

ORIGIN: Native

ECONOMIC VALUE: Wildlife - fair   Livestock - fair

Also known as "yellow puff" and "yellow sensitivebriar", this plant is sensitive and closes it's leaves upon touch or when the weather is cloudy. It has been used for erosion control on sandy sites. The plant may be propagated vegetatively or from seeds.

GROWTH CHARACTERISTICS:

forb, 20-40 cm (8-16 in) tall; stems prostrate to decumbent; reproduces by seeds

DISTINGUISHING CHARACTERISTICS:

Leaves: alternate, bipinnately compound, petiole without glands; stipules lanceolate, well-developed; pinnae in 2-10 pairs; leaflets, 8-16 per pinna, veination reticulate

Flowers: small in round to elongated heads, 25-50 flowers; sepals 5-parted; petals 5-parted, yellow; stamens 10

Fruit: legume, 1-5 cm (3/8-2 in) long, 5-15 mm (3/16-9/16 in) wide, flattened; seeds elongated

LIVESTOCK LOSSES:

HABITAT:

sandy areas, frequently dry; scattered in the eastern part of the State. Texas distribution: Areas 2-5

Pisum sativum
Austrian winterpea

AUSTRIAN WINTERPEA

Legume Family (Fabaceae)

LATIN NAME:	*Pisum sativum* L. (includes *P. arvense* L.)
LONGEVITY:	Annual
SEASON:	Cool
ORIGIN:	Introduced
ECONOMIC VALUE:	Wildlife - fair Livestock - fair

Native to Europe this introduced species is a winter annual, planted because of its high protein content. Austrian winterpea is grown for hay, silage, and pasture.

GROWTH CHARACTERISTICS:

forb, to 200 cm (6 ft) long; stems glabrous; reproduces by seeds

DISTINGUISHING CHARACTERISTICS:

Leaves: alternate, pinnately compound; leaflets glabrous, 1-3 pair, 2-7 cm (3/4-2 3/4 in) long, 1-4 cm (3/8-1 1/2 in) wide, oblong to suborbicular; stipules to 10 cm (4 in) long and 6 cm (2 3/8 in) wide

Flowers: racemes with 1-3 flowers; corolla white to purple, 15-35 mm (9/16-1 3/8 in) long

Fruit: legume, 3-12 cm (1 1/4-4 3/4 in) long, 10-25 mm (3/8-1 in) wide with up to 10 seeds, yellow to brownish

LIVESTOCK LOSSES:

HABITAT:

cultivated for winter forage. Texas distribution: Areas 1-8, 10

Prosopis glandulosa
honey mesquite
(Stubbendieck et al., 1982)

HONEY MESQUITE

Legume Family (Fabaceae)

LATIN NAME: *Prosopis glandulosa* Torr.

LONGEVITY: Perennial

SEASON: Warm

ORIGIN: Native

ECONOMIC VALUE: Wildlife - fair   Livestock - poor

Mesquite, one of the hardier plants in Texas, has no known insect or disease pests and propagates readily by seeds or sprouting from its crown. It is capable of reaching water supplies far below the surface and out of reach of many other plants. The wood burns very hot and is prized for barbecue cooking. The beans are very high in protein and utilized readily by wildlife and domestic livestock. Indians ground the beans into flour and boiled them to extract a tea.

GROWTH CHARACTERISTICS:

> shrub to small tree, 1-4 m (3-13 ft) tall, usually much branched at the base; initiates growth in March or April, flowers in May, fruits mature in August; growth controlled by moisture availability and temperature; reproduces by seeds and basal shoots

DISTINGUISHING CHARACTERISTICS:

Leaves: compound, bipinnate, deciduous; leaflets in pairs of 6-30, linear to oblong, 3-5 cm (1 1/4-2 in) long, glabrous; stipules modified to spines

Flowers: in racemes, elongate, yellow; pedicels glandular

Fruit: legume, 10-20 cm (4-8 in) long, linear, slightly curved, slight constriction between seeds

Other: stems armed with stipular spines to 5 cm (2 in) long; spines rigid, straight; stems zig-zag

LIVESTOCK LOSSES:

> large amounts of this as a forage may result in rumen stasis

HABITAT:

> plains and prairies; especially on disturbed sites. Texas distribution: Areas 2-10

Psoralea tenuiflora
scurfpea

SCURFPEA

Legume Family (Fabaceae)

LATIN NAME: *Psoralea tenuiflora* Pursh

LONGEVITY: Perennial

SEASON: Warm

ORIGIN: Native

ECONOMIC VALUE: Wildlife - good   Livestock - fair

Scurfpea owes it's common name to the small glands on the stem and leaves that lend the plant a rough or "scurfy" appearance upon close examination. It is also known as "wild alfalfa".

GROWTH CHARACTERISTICS:

forb, 20-50 cm (8-20 in) tall, much branched above; reproduces by seeds and long rootstocks; highly drought resistant

DISTINGUISHING CHARACTERISTICS:

Leaves: alternate, palmately compound, usually 3 (occasionally 5) leaflets; leaflets 1-4 cm (3/8-1 1/2 in) long, linear to oblanceolate, pubescent above and nearly glabrous below, surfaces glandular dotted

Flowers: solitary to 3 per node; calyx tube glandular, 2-2.5 mm (about 1/16 in) long; corolla blue to purple, 4-7 mm (5/32-1/4 in) long

Fruit: legume, 5-8 mm (3/16-5/16 in) long, ovoid with a short straight beak, gland dotted

Other: stem readily disarticulates from the crown at maturity

LIVESTOCK LOSSES:

reported to be poisonous to cattle and horses but without confirmation; may cause bloat

HABITAT:

prairies, plains, and open woods. Texas distribution: Areas 2-5, 7-10

Schrankia uncinata
catclaw sensitivebriar

CATCLAW SENSITIVEBRIAR

Legume Family (Fabaceae)

LATIN NAME:	*Schrankia uncinata* Willd.
LONGEVITY:	Perennial
SEASON:	Warm
ORIGIN:	Native
ECONOMIC VALUE:	Wildlife - good Livestock - good

The common name "sensitivebriar" and another less common name "shameboy" refer to the habit of this forb to tightly close it's leaves upon a touch. It is a valuable, high protein forage for wildlife and would probably be used more if not for the "catclaws" on the stem.

GROWTH CHARACTERISTICS:

> forb, 60-200 cm (24-79 in) long; stem weak, prostrate, armed with recurved prickles; reproduces by seeds

DISTINGUISHING CHARACTERISTICS:

Leaves: alternate, pinnately compound, stipules subulate; leaflets 8-16 pairs, 4-8 mm (5/32-5/16 in) long, elliptical, caudate

Flowers: inflorescence of globose heads, pink, diameter 11-25 mm (3/8-1 in); stamens 8-12

Fruit: legume, 5-10 cm (2-4 in) long, diameter 3-4 mm (1/8-5/32 in), prickly

LIVESTOCK LOSSES:

> none

HABITAT:

> common in sandy soils. Texas distribution: Areas 1-5, 8, 9

Trifolium incarnatum
crimson clover

CRIMSON CLOVER

Legume Family (Fabaceae)

LATIN NAME: *Trifolium incarnatum* L.

LONGEVITY: Annual

SEASON: Cool

ORIGIN: Introduced

ECONOMIC VALUE: Wildlife - fair   Livestock - good

Crimson clover is an excellent late winter forage for both domestic livestock and wildlife because it is high in protein when most choice forage plants are not available. The State Highway Department has utilized crimson clover for erosion control plantings.

GROWTH CHARACTERISTICS:

forb, 20-70 cm (8-28 in) long; stems ascending; reproduces by seeds

DISTINGUISHING CHARACTERISTICS:

Leaves: alternate, compound, palmately trifoliate; petioles 5-25 cm (2-10 in) long; stipules fused to petiole base, to 2 cm (3/4 in) long; leaflets 1-3.5 cm (3/8-1 3/8 in) long, rhombic orbicular to obovate

Flowers: inflorescence in racemose clusters; calyx tubular, 3-5 mm (1/8-3/16 in) long, 10-nerved; corolla papilionaceous, 8-12 mm (5/16-1/2 in) long, red or scarlet

Fruit: legume, ovoid

Other: showy spring flower

LIVESTOCK LOSSES:

HABITAT:

escaped cultivation to grow on roadsides and other disturbed sites. Texas distribution: Areas 1-4

Trifolium repens
white clover

WHITE CLOVER

Legume Family (Fabaceae)

LATIN NAME: *Trifolium repens* L.

LONGEVITY: Perennial

SEASON: Cool

ORIGIN: Introduced

ECONOMIC VALUE: Wildlife - fair   Livestock - good

Also known as "Dutch white clover" owing to it's origins in Europe, white clover is an important early season source of pollen for bees. It is a common lawn weed and valuable whitetail deer forage.

GROWTH CHARACTERISTICS:

forb, 10-30 cm (4-12 in) long; stems creeping (rooting at nodes), matforming; reproduces by seeds and vegetative reproduction

DISTINGUISHING CHARACTERISTICS:

Leaves: alternate, compound, palmately trifoliate; petioles 5-15 cm (2-6 in) long; stipules adnate to petiole base; leaflets 1-3 cm (3/8-1 3/4 in) long, obovate to obcordate

Flowers: peduncle 10-30 cm (4-12 in) long; inflorescence capitate (nearly globose), diameter to 2.3 cm (1 in) wide; calyx 5-parted, lobes shorter than tube; corolla papilionaceous, 7-11 mm (1/4-1/2 in) long, white (rarely pinkish)

Fruit: legume, 4-6 mm (5/32-1/4 in) long, oblong, 3-4 seeded

LIVESTOCK LOSSES:

HABITAT:

widely introduced and occasionally escaping along roadsides. Texas distribution: Areas 1-7

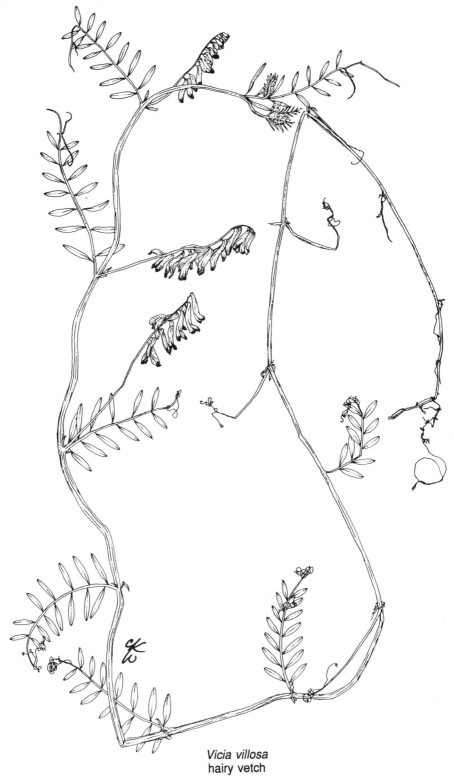

Vicia villosa
hairy vetch

HAIRY VETCH

Legume Family (Fabaceae)

LATIN NAME: *Vicia villosa* Roth

LONGEVITY: Annual

SEASON: Cool

ORIGIN: Introduced

ECONOMIC VALUE: Wildlife - fair   Livestock - good

A native of Europe, hairy vetch is a valuable forage for whitetail deer.

GROWTH CHARACTERISTICS:

> forb, 20-100 cm (8-39 in) long; stems prostrate to spreading; reproduces by seeds

DISTINGUISHING CHARACTERISTICS:

Leaves: alternate, pinnately compound; stipules leaf-like; leaflets 10-18, oblong to linear, obtuse to acute to mucronate

Flowers: in dense racemes with 12-45 flowers; flowers papilionaceous, 10-20 mm (3/8-3/4 in) long; calyx with 5 unequal teeth; corolla violet and white or pinkish white

Fruit: legume, 2-3 cm (3/4-1 1/4 in) long, 6-9 mm (1/4-11/32 in) wide, oblong, apex oblique

LIVESTOCK LOSSES:

> none

HABITAT:

> common along roadsides in disturbed habitats. Texas distribution: Areas 4, 5

Rhus aromatica
skunkbush
(Forest Service, 1937)

SKUNKBUSH

Sumac Family (Anacardiaceae)

LATIN NAME: *Rhus aromatica* Ait.
                         (*Rhus trilobata* Nutt.)

LONGEVITY: Perennial

SEASON: Warm

ORIGIN: Native

ECONOMIC VALUE: Wildlife - good   Livestock - good

Skunkbush owes it's common name to the foul odor released when the vegetation is crushed. It is one of the sumacs and occurs throughout the United States and Mexico. Sumacs are not bothered greatly by disease, insects, or drought, which perhaps accounts for their wide distribution. Quail and pheasant feed on the fruits of skunkbush. The leaves were brewed into a soothing tea by early people.

GROWTH CHARACTERISTICS:

shrub, to 2.5 m (8 ft) tall, flowers before leaves appear in the spring; reproduces by seeds

DISTINGUISHING CHARACTERISTICS:

Leaves: alternate; compound, trifoliate, pale beneath, sessile, terminal leaflet longer; leaflets 2-6 cm (3/4-2 3/8 in) long, bases cuneate

Flowers: in clusters near branch apex; corolla pale yellow to cream colored

Fruit: drupe, 6-7 mm (about 1/4 in) wide, red or reddish orange, glandular pubescent, in dense clusters

LIVESTOCK LOSSES:

HABITAT:

shallow rocky sites to stream sides and canyons. Texas distribution: Areas 4, 5, 7, 8, 10

Rhus copallina
flameleaf sumac

FLAMELEAF SUMAC

Sumac Family (Anacardiaceae)

LATIN NAME: *Rhus copallina* L.

LONGEVITY: Perennial

SEASON: Warm

ORIGIN: Native

ECONOMIC VALUE: Wildlife - good (birds)   Livestock - poor

The striking red leaves in the autumn lend the common name to flameleaf sumac. It forms thickets that are readily visible in autumn. Indians added crushed flameleaf sumac fruits to water to improve the taste of the water. They also mixed the leaves with tobacco and smoked the concoction.

GROWTH CHARACTERISTICS:

shrub or tree, to 10 m (32 ft) tall, numerous lenticels on older stems, young branches tomentose; buds light brown; reproduces by seeds

DISTINGUISHING CHARACTERISTICS:

Leaves: alternate, compound, pinnate, 15-38 cm (6-15 in) long, petiole 3-6 cm (1 1/4-2 3/8 in) long; leaflets 7-11, moistly sessile, to 8 cm (3 1/8 in) long, to 4 cm (1 1/2 in) wide, elliptical to lanceolate, glabrous and shiny above, lower surface glandular hairs and dull; margins entire to serrate; rachis winged

Flowers: inflorescence a thyrse, 10-14 cm (4-5 1/2 in) long, about 10 cm (4 in) wide; flowers greenish white

Fruit: drupe, 4 mm (5/32 in) in diameter, slightly flattened, with glandular red hairs; seed diameter 2-2.5 mm (about 1/16 in), smooth to rough

LIVESTOCK LOSSES:

HABITAT:

rocky hills, woods and bottomlands. Texas distribution: Areas 1-7

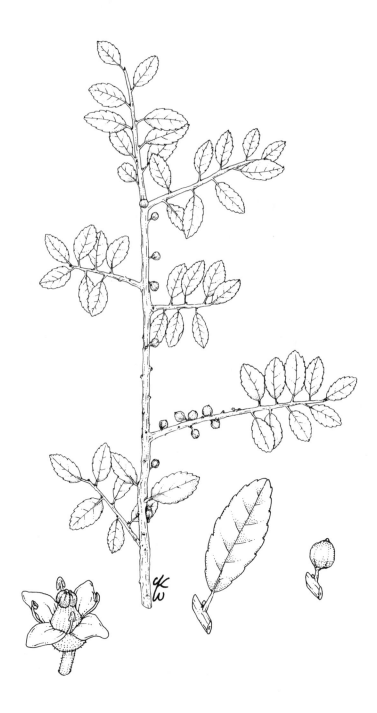

Ilex vomitoria
yaupon

YAUPON

Holly Family (Aquifoliaceae)

LATIN NAME: *Ilex vomitoria* Ait.

LONGEVITY: Perennial

SEASON: Cool-Warm (Evergreen)

ORIGIN: Native

ECONOMIC VALUE: Wildlife - good   Livestock - fair

"Yaupon holly", thus named because of it's holly-like appearance of evergreen leaves and bright red berries, has found a place as a popular ornamental plant. In it's native habitat, it is browsed by whitetail deer. The species name "vomitoria" refers to early uses of the plant, particularly the leaves, for medicinal teas.

GROWTH CHARACTERISTICS:

dioecious shrub, 1-8 m (3-26 ft) tall, much branched from the base upward, forms dense thickets; flowers April to May; reproduces by sprouts as well as seeds

DISTINGUISHING CHARACTERISTICS:

Leaves: simple, alternate; blades 2-4 cm (3/4-1 1/2 in) long, elliptic to oval, margins crenate, dark glands on margins, dark green above, pale green below; petiole 1-3 mm (1/32-1/8 in) long

Flowers: unisexual, white; staminate flowers in dense clusters, pistillate flowers few in number; some flowers perfect

Fruit: drupe, 5-8 mm (3/16-5/16 in) long, bright red, four-seeded

Other: stem light gray to whitish; bark thin

LIVESTOCK LOSSES:

HABITAT:

sandy woodlands, stream and pond margins. Texas distribution: Areas 1-3, 6, 7

Asclepias latifolia
broadleaf milkweed

BROADLEAF MILKWEED

Milkweed Family (Asclepiadaceae)

LATIN NAME: *Asclepias latifolia* (Torr.) Raf.

LONGEVITY: Perennial

SEASON: Warm

ORIGIN: Native

ECONOMIC VALUE: Wildlife - poor   Livestock - poor (poisonous)

"Asclepias" is for "Asklepios" the Greek God of Medicine. Like other milkweeds, the common name refers to the milky sap exuded upon breaking the stem, leaves, or roots. Early desert peoples used the plant medicinally. The tender shoots are edible.

GROWTH CHARACTERISTICS:

forb; stems erect, usually unbranched, 20-90 cm (8-35 in) tall, minutely tomentose, becoming glabrate; flowers May to September; reproduces by seeds

DISTINGUISHING CHARACTERISTICS:

Leaves: simple, opposite, short petiolate; blades 4-16 cm (1 1/2-6 1/4 in) long, 4-14 cm (1 1/2-5 1/2 in) wide, broadly oval to ovate, base somewhat cordate; glaucous; petiole about 5 mm (3/16 in) long

Flowers: in lateral inflorescences at upper nodes; flower large, calyx 5-parted; corolla pale green, reflexed, lobes about 12 mm (1/2 in) long

Fruit: follicles, erect or deflexed, 6-8 cm (2 3/8-3 1/8 in) long, 1-3 cm (3/8-1 1/4 in) wide, broadly fusiform, smooth, nearly glabrous; seeds oval, 7 mm (1/4 in) long, coma 2 cm (3/4 in) long

LIVESTOCK LOSSES:

0.5% of the body weight of the animal has killed cattle; 0.15% of the body weight has killed sheep and goats; the poisons include cardiac and steroid glucocides

HABITAT:

badlands, prairies, disturbed pastures, roadsides. Texas distribution: Areas 7-10

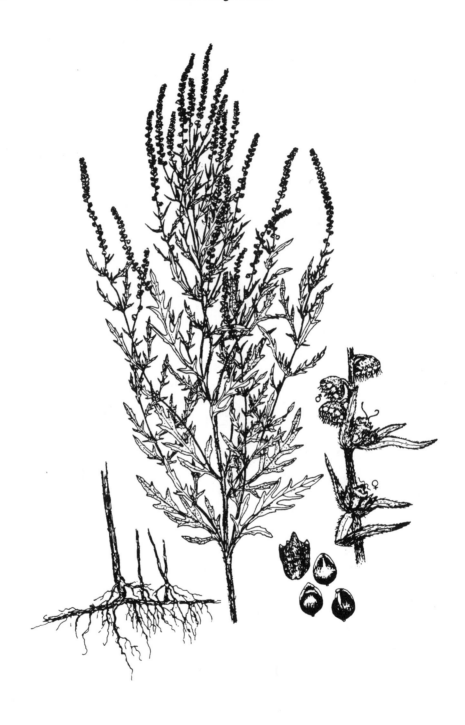

Ambrosia psilostachya
western ragweed
(Stubbendieck et al., 1982)

WESTERN RAGWEED

Sunflower Family (Asteraceae)

LATIN NAME: *Ambrosia psilostachya* DC.

LONGEVITY: Perennial

SEASON: Warm

ORIGIN: Native

ECONOMIC VALUE: Wildlife - good   Livestock - poor

Probably the most famous allergy plant, western ragweed grows in a variety of habitats throughout western North America. It's pollen is very light and easily air borne to the chagrin of those with allergies. Instead of relying upon bees for pollination, the plant depends upon the wind to carry it's pollen from plant to plant.

GROWTH CHARACTERISTICS:

monoecious forb, 25-75 cm (10-30 in) tall; forms extensive colonies from creeping rhizomes; reproduces by seeds

DISTINGUISHING CHARACTERISTICS:

Leaves: opposite, simple; 3-12 cm (1 1/4-4 3/4 in) long, deeply narrow-lobed to linear-lanceolate divisions; sessile or nearly so, covered with short stiff hairs

Flowers: heads small and yellow green; staminate flowers in terminal racemes, anthers yellow; female flowers axillary; inflorescence much branched

Fruit: achene with woody hull subtended by short spines

LIVESTOCK LOSSES:

may accumulate nitrates; gives cows milk a bitter taste

HABITAT:

disturbed sites, dry prairies, hills. Texas distribution: Areas 1-10

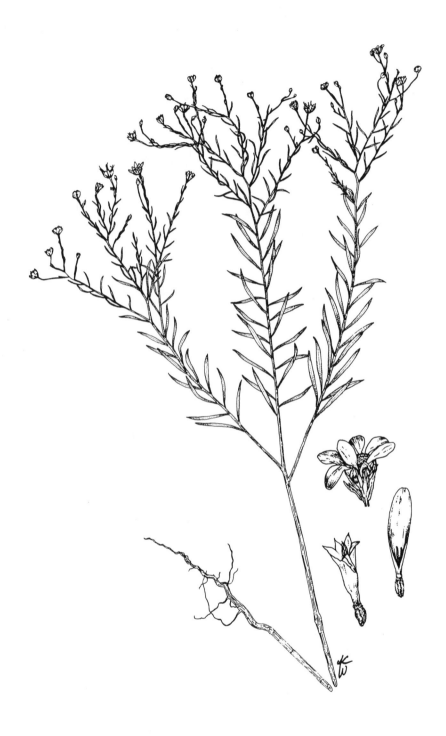

Amphiachyris dracunculoides
common broomweed

COMMON BROOMWEED

Sunflower Family (Asteraceae)

LATIN NAME: *Amphiachyris dracunculoides* DC.
                                (*Xanthocephalum dracunculoides* (DC.) Shinners)

LONGEVITY: Annual

SEASON: Warm

ORIGIN: Native

ECONOMIC VALUE: Wildlife - poor   Livestock - poor

Early settlers used the dried plants as brooms. By the time the plant flowers, the leaves have usually dried and dropped off. It is a very conspicuous fall flower and the flowers dry well.

GROWTH CHARACTERISTICS:

forb, 20-60 cm (8-24 in) tall, simple below and much branched in the upper half; flowers September to November; reproduces by seeds

DISTINGUISHING CHARACTERISTICS:

Leaves: alternate, simple, sessile, 1.8-7 cm (11/16-2 3/4 in) long, 0.5-5 mm (less than 1/32-3/16 in) wide, linear to narrowly elliptic, resinous, glabrous

Flowers: heads numerous, crowded; involucre 3-5 mm (1/8-3/16 in) long; ray flowers yellow, fertile; disk flowers yellow, sterile; phyllary bracts firm, straw-colored with green-tips

Fruit: achenes, 1.5 mm (1/16 in) long, pappus of slender membranous scales

Other: pungent odor

LIVESTOCK LOSSES:

herbage and pollen can cause an itchy dermatitis in livestock and humans

HABITAT:

dry prairies, limestone barrens, disturbed sites. Texas distribution: Areas 2-5, 8-10

Artemisia filifolia
sand sagebrush

SAND SAGEBRUSH

Sunflower Family (Asteraceae)

LATIN NAME: *Artemisia filifolia* Torr.

LONGEVITY: Perennial

SEASON: Warm

ORIGIN: Native

ECONOMIC VALUE: Wildlife - poor   Livestock - poor

Also known as "wormwood", the pollen from all the sages is very allergenic. The species name "filifolia" refers to the filiform or threadlike leaves. The plant has been used medicinally, primarily to treat stomach and intestinal disorders.

GROWTH CHARACTERISTICS:

> shrub, 0.5-1 m (20-39 in) tall, much branched; starts growth in April to May, flowers throughout the growing season; reproduces by seeds

DISTINGUISHING CHARACTERISTICS:

Leaves: simple, alternate, 3.5-7.5 cm (1 3/8-3 in) long, sessile, filiform, lower leaves 3-parted, upper leaves entire

Flowers: in dense leafy panicles; heads discoid, gray-green

Fruit: achene without a pappus

Other: twigs striate, pubescent when young, glabrate with age

LIVESTOCK LOSSES:

> may cause "sage sickness" in horses

HABITAT:

> sandy soil; generally an indicator of deep sand. Texas distribution: Areas 8-10

Artemisia ludoviciana
Mexican sagewort
(Forest Service, 1937)

MEXICAN SAGEWORT

Sunflower Family (Asteraceae)

LATIN NAME: *Artemisia ludoviciana* Nutt.

LONGEVITY: Perennial

SEASON: Warm

ORIGIN: Native

ECONOMIC VALUE: Wildlife - poor   Livestock - good

An aromatic forb, Mexican sagewort is related to the well known sagebrushes. This plant is widely distributed throughout western North America and is generally recognized to have several varieties that are very similar. It is also known as "cudweed sagewort" and "Louisiana wormwood".

GROWTH CHARACTERISTICS:

> forb, 30-100 cm (12-39 in) long, erect; reproduces in colonies from extensive root-stocks and seeds

DISTINGUISHING CHARACTERISTICS:

Leaves: alternate, simple; 2-12 cm (3/4-4 3/4 in) long, 3-10 mm (1/8-3/8 in) wide, linear to oblanceolate, margins entire to toothed, white tomentose

Flowers: heads small, 3-4 mm (1/8-5/32 in) wide, discoid, gray or white-woolly

Fruit: achenes, less than 1 mm (1/32 in) long, pappus absent

LIVESTOCK LOSSES:

> none

HABITAT:

> prairies and hills. Texas distribution: Areas 1-10

Aster subulatus var. *ligulatus*
slim aster

SLIM ASTER

Sunflower Family (Asteraceae)

LATIN NAME: *Aster subulatus* Michx. var. *ligulatus* Shinners

LONGEVITY: Annual

SEASON: Warm

ORIGIN: Native

ECONOMIC VALUE: Wildlife - fair   Livestock - fair

Common where extra moisture is present, slim aster is a very prolific weed in lawns and is often found in playa lakes. "Aster" is a Greek word meaning "star" referring to the flowers of slim aster. Other names for the plant include "annual aster" and "hierba del marrano".

GROWTH CHARACTERISTICS:

forb, 10-70 cm (4-28 in) tall; stems much branched, robust; reproduces by seeds

DISTINGUISHING CHARACTERISTICS:

Leaves: alternate, simple, sessile, 1-15 cm (3/8-6 in) long, 2-6 mm (1/16-1/4 in) wide, linear, margins entire (rarely serrate)

Flowers: inflorescence a head; phyllaries linear, in several series; heads with ray and disk flowers; pappus of capillary bristles in 1-series, similar in both flower types; ray flowers white or bluish white; disk flowers yellowish; ligules longer than disk flowers, purple to pink or white

Fruit: achenes, 2-3 mm (1/16-1/8 in) long, pubescent, light brown

LIVESTOCK LOSSES:

HABITAT:

weed on the margins of ditches, lakes, and streams; common in poorly drained sites. Texas distribution: Areas 1-10

Baccharis salicina
willow baccharis

WILLOW BACCHARIS

Sunflower Family (Asteraceae)

LATIN NAME: *Baccharis salicina* T. & G.

LONGEVITY: Perennial

SEASON: Warm

ORIGIN: Native

ECONOMIC VALUE: Wildlife - poor   Livestock - poor

Named because it resembles willow (genus: Salix), willow baccharis commonly occurs along streambanks as does willow. Another common name for the shrub is "groundsel tree".

GROWTH CHARACTERISTICS:

dioecious shrub; 1-3 m (3-11 in) tall; branchlets angled, striate, glabrous; reproduces by seeds

DISTINGUISHING CHARACTERISTICS:

Leaves: nearly sessile, alternate, simple; blades 3-6 cm (1 1/4-2 3/8 in) long, 4-12 mm (5/32-1/2 in) wide, broader leaves 3-nerved, oblong to oblanceolate

Flowers: unisexual; pistillate heads with 20-30 flowers; phyllaries ovate to lanceolate, apex acute to obtuse and reddish brown, margins scarious and erose; receptacle flat, naked; disk flowers 5-parted, yellowish-white, 3-4 mm (about 1/8 in) long; pappus of 2 series of bristles, 12 mm (1/2 in) long; staminate head with phyllaries like pistillate flowers; disk flowers 3-4.5 mm (1/8-3/16 in) long (ray flowers absent), white to yellowish-brown; pappus equals corolla length, apex plumose

Fruit: achenes, 1-2 mm (1/32-1/16 in) long, glabrous, 8-10-nerved

LIVESTOCK LOSSES:

suspected of being poisonous

HABITAT:

most frequent in highly disturbed sites, roadsides, calcareous to sandy soils, one of the first shrubs to come back in secondary succession. Texas distribution: Areas 2-9

Engelmannia pinnatifida
engelmanndaisy

ENGELMANNDAISY

Sunflower Family (Asteraceae)

LATIN NAME: *Engelmannia pinnatifida* Nutt.

LONGEVITY: Perennial

SEASON: Cool

ORIGIN: Native

ECONOMIC VALUE: Wildlife - good   Livestock - good

Engelmanndaisy, widely distributed along roadsides in Texas, bears blooms for two months or more. It can be grown from seed or by transplanting the crown of the plant. The name honors George Engelmann (1809-1884) who collected and studied plants extensively in Texas.

GROWTH CHARACTERISTICS:

forb, 20-80 cm (8-31 in) tall, stem single or bunched, hispid; reproduces by seeds

DISTINGUISHING CHARACTERISTICS:

Leaves: simple, alternate; basal leaves 10-30 cm (4-12 in) long, once pinnatifid; stem leaves 8-32 cm (3 1/8-13 in) long, deeply pinnatifid, hispid

Flowers: branches terminate in a head inflorescence, involucre 6-12 mm (1/4-1/2 in) long, phyllaries in 3 series; ray flowers, about 1 cm (3/8 in) long, yellow, usually 8, apex 3-toothed, pistillate, pappus of a few deciduous scales; disk flowers perfect but infertile, yellow, apex 5-toothed

Fruit: achenes flattened, obovate

LIVESTOCK LOSSES:

HABITAT:

prairies, upland sites, or open roadsides. Texas distribution: Areas 2-10

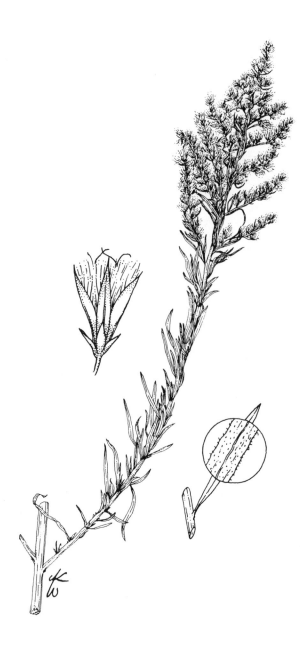

Eupatorium compositifolium
yankeeweed

YANKEEWEED

Sunflower Family (Asteraceae)

LATIN NAME: *Eupatorium compositifolium* Walt.

LONGEVITY: Perennial

SEASON: Warm

ORIGIN: Native

ECONOMIC VALUE: Wildlife - poor   Livestock - poor

Yankeeweed appears as a cluster of thick green finely divided leaves until September when it sends up a flowering stalk covered with similar leaves. Pleasant smelling flowers appear very late in the fall. The plant has been used to control wind erosion on sand dunes. Dividing old plants is the most effective method of propagating yankeeweed.

GROWTH CHARACTERISTICS:

> forb; stems to 3 m (11 ft) tall, erect, coarsely pubescent; reproduces by seeds and rhizomes

DISTINGUISHING CHARACTERISTICS:

Leaves: mostly alternate, simple, crowded; 1 or 2 pinnately divided, fine segments 1-2 mm (1/32-1/16 in) wide

Flowers: heads in a panicle-like arrangement, green to bronze colored; heads 3-5 flowered; phyllaries in two series; corolla white

Fruit: achenes, 1.5-2 mm (about 1/16 in) long

LIVESTOCK LOSSES:

> none

HABITAT:

> frequent in disturbed sites on sandy soils of the eastern side of Texas. Texas distribution: Areas 1-3, 6

Grindelia squarrosa
curlycup gumweed
(Stubbendieck et al., 1982)

CURLYCUP GUMWEED

Sunflower Family (Asteraceae)

LATIN NAME: *Grindelia squarrosa* (Pursh) Dun.

LONGEVITY: Perennial

SEASON: Warm

ORIGIN: Native

ECONOMIC VALUE: Wildlife - poor   Livestock - fair

Curlycup gumweed was chewed as a gum by early peoples. The entire plant was used in remedies for skin irritations, stomach and kidney disorders. It is also known by a variety of common names: yerba del buey, gumweed, rosinweed, and tarweed.

GROWTH CHARACTERISTICS:

> forb, 20-90 cm (8-35 in) tall, erect, from a taproot; starts growth in late spring, flowers in July to August; reproduces by seeds

DISTINGUISHING CHARACTERISTICS:

Leaves: alternate, simple; 2-5 cm (3/4-2 in) long, margins serrulate with gland-dotted teeth, glands in the sinus; sessile and somewhat clasping

Flowers: radiate heads, 2-3 cm (3/4-1 1/4 in) wide, yellow; rays may be lacking; phyllary bracts imbricate with tips squarrose, resinous

Fruit: achenes, glabrous; pappus of stiff deciduous awns

LIVESTOCK LOSSES:

> may accumulate selenium

HABITAT:

> waste places, disturbed sites. Texas distribution: Areas 5, 7-9

Gutierrezia sarothrae
broom snakeweed
(Forest Service, 1937)

BROOM SNAKEWEED

Sunflower Family (Asteraceae)

LATIN NAME: *Gutierrezia sarothrae* (Pursh) Shinners
(*Xanthocephalum sarothrae* (Pursh) Britt. & Rusby)

LONGEVITY: Perennial

SEASON: Warm

ORIGIN: Native

ECONOMIC VALUE: Wildlife - fair   Livestock - poor (poisonous)

Broom snakeweed has been the subject of much research in the southwestern U.S. where scientists believe it is the cause of the greatest economic loss on rangeland to the livestock industry. Also know as "turpentine weed", it is broom-like in appearance lending to the common name.

GROWTH CHARACTERISTICS:

suffrutescent shrub, 10-55 cm (4-22 in) tall, much branched from the base; leaves deciduous at the base of plant; reproduces by seeds

DISTINGUISHING CHARACTERISTICS:

Leaves: alternate, simple, sessile, linear to filiform, 2-4 cm (3/4-1 1/2 in) long, 1-2 mm (1/32-1/16 in) wide, pubescent to scabrous, margins entire, rolled inward

Flowers: inflorescence a head, cylindrical; heads arranged in cymes, yellow; phyllary bracts imbricate and may be green-tipped; flowers radiate

Fruit: achene, pappus of chaffy scales

Other: subshrub with slender herbaceous stems above and woody stems toward the plant base

LIVESTOCK LOSSES:

saponin, the poison causes death or abortion in cattle and sheep

HABITAT:

indicates overgrazing; rocky and dry plains and hillsides, on many soil types. Texas distribution: Areas 2, 5, 7-10

Helenium amarum
bitter sneezeweed

BITTER SNEEZEWEED

Sunflower Family (Asteraceae)

LATIN NAME: *Helenium amarum* (Raf.) Rock.

LONGEVITY: Annual

SEASON: Warm

ORIGIN: Native

ECONOMIC VALUE: Wildlife - poor   Livestock - poor (poisonous)

Milk from cows grazing bitter sneezeweed and honey from bees utilizing the plant are both bitter and distasteful. The common name "sneezeweed" is given to a group of plants whose pollens are very allergenic.

GROWTH CHARACTERISTICS:

forb; stems 20-70 cm (8-28 in) tall, erect, unbranched at the base, branching above the middle of the stem, stem ribbed; reproduces by seeds

DISTINGUISHING CHARACTERISTICS:

Leaves: alternate, simple, sessile, ascending; blades linear or pinnately dissected, glabrous

Flowers: numerous heads; ray flowers usually 8, yellow; disk flowers 5-lobed, yellow

Fruit: achene

Other: leaves, stems, and flowers contain a bitter tasting resin that is also odoriferous

LIVESTOCK LOSSES:

sheep, cattle, goats, and horses can become weak, develop diarrhea, vomit, and bloat. The animal's pulse is irregular and breathing is rapid. The plant causes gastroenteritis in the stomach.

HABITAT:

all disturbed sites in the eastern half of the state, dense stands indicate a highly disturbed site. Texas distribution: Areas 1-8

Helianthus maximiliani
Maximilian sunflower
(Wasser, 1982)

MAXIMILIAN SUNFLOWER

Sunflower Family (Asteraceae)

LATIN NAME: *Helianthus maximiliani* Schrad.

LONGEVITY: Perennial

SEASON: Warm

ORIGIN: Native

ECONOMIC VALUE: Wildlife - fair   Livestock - fair

Maximilian sunflower is named for Prince Maximilian of Wied Neuwied, who led an expedition into the west in the 1830's. The plant is a prolific seed producer, making it a valuable food source for wild birds. Deer also utilize the plant. The tubers were important foods for some tribes of Indians. Maximilian sunflower produces many annual stalks from a perennial root base. It has been in cultivation for many years and is used in land reclamation.

GROWTH CHARACTERISTICS:

forb, 0.3-3 m (1-11 ft) tall; reproduces from seeds or from crown or woody rootstock

DISTINGUISHING CHARACTERISTICS:

Leaves: simple, alternate, 14-30 cm (5 1/2-12 in) long, 2-5 cm (3/4-2 in) wide, lanceolate, acuminate at base and apex, margins entire to serrate, gray-green

Flowers: heads in racemose arrangements, 5-8 cm (2-3 1/8 in) wide; phyllaries 10-15 mm (3/8-9/16 in) long, dense, pubescent; ray flowers bright yellow, 2-4 cm (3/4-1 1/2 in) long, obscurely 3-toothed; disk flowers 10-12 mm (3/8-1/2 in) long, yellowish

Fruit: achene

LIVESTOCK LOSSES:

HABITAT:

moist ditches or depressions; prairies. Texas distribution: Areas 2-5, 7-9

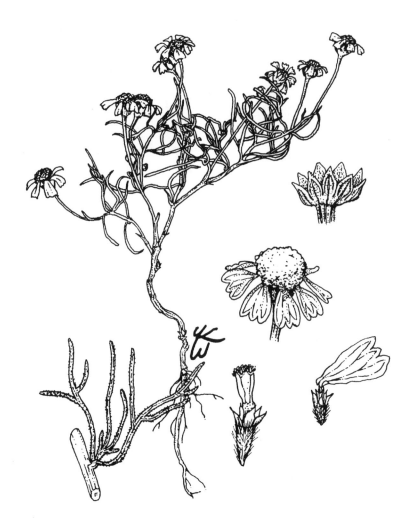

Hymenoxys odorata
western bitterweed

WESTERN BITTERWEED

Sunflower Family (Asteraceae)

LATIN NAME: *Hymenoxys odorata* DC.

LONGEVITY: Annual

SEASON: Cool

ORIGIN: Native

ECONOMIC VALUE: Wildlife - poor   Livestock - poor (poisonous)

The foliage of western bitterweed is dotted with small glands and a resinlike substance which makes the plant bitter to the taste. These also emit a foul odor when the foliage is crushed.

GROWTH CHARACTERISTICS:

forb, 7-40 cm (2 3/4-16 in) tall, much branched from base; germinates in mid to late winter; reproduces by seeds

DISTINGUISHING CHARACTERISTICS:

Leaves: simple, alternate, 3-6 cm (1 1/4-2 3/8 in) long, pinnately divided into 3-15 linear divisions, glandular punctate, aromatic when crushed

Flowers: in small heads, 0.3-1.2 cm (1/8-1/2 in) wide, corymbose; ray flower yellow, corolla 3-lobed; disk flowers yellow; outer phyllary bracts united to near the base

Fruit: achenes; pappus scales acuminate

Other: plant body glabrate to slightly pubescent

LIVESTOCK LOSSES:

poisonous to sheep in winter; toxicity increases with drought conditions, poison cumulative; poison is water soluble

HABITAT:

disturbed sites in pastures, range, or roadways. Texas distribution: Areas 6-10

Liatris punctata
dotted gayfeather

DOTTED GAYFEATHER

Sunflower Family (Asteraceae)

LATIN NAME: *Liatris punctata* Hook.

LONGEVITY: Perennial

SEASON: Warm

ORIGIN: Native

ECONOMIC VALUE: Wildlife - fair   Livestock - fair

Also known as "blazing star", dotted gayfeather is one of the showiest natives on the prairies. The roots and corms of the plant reportedly have been used to treat sore throats and rattlesnake bites. Available from commercial nurserymen, dotted gayfeather is fairly easy to transplant in the autumn.

GROWTH CHARACTERISTICS:

> forb, 20-70 cm (8-28 in) tall, single to multiple stemmed at the plant base; flowers August to October; grows from the bulb-like caudex; reproduces by seeds

DISTINGUISHING CHARACTERISTICS:

Leaves: alternate, linear, rigid; basal leaves 8-15 cm (3 1/8-6 in) long, 1.5-5 mm (1/16-3/16 in) wide, ciliate to scabrous, surface glabrous and punctate

Flowers: heads in a spike-like arrangement, spike 7-25 cm (2 3/4-10 in) long; heads 1.4-2 cm (9/16-3/4 in) long, discoid, ray flowers purple; phyllary bracts thick, punctate

Fruit: achenes, 6-7 mm (about 1/4 in) long, ribbed, pubescent; pappus plumose

Other: crown is a bulb-like corm

LIVESTOCK LOSSES:

> none

HABITAT:

> dry prairies and hills. Texas distribution: Areas 8-10

Ratibida columnifera
upright prairie-coneflower
(Wasser, 1982)

UPRIGHT PRAIRIE-CONEFLOWER

Sunflower Family (Asteraceae)

LATIN NAME: *Ratibida columnifera* (Nutt.) Woot. & Standl.
                    (*Ratibida columnaris* (Sims) D. Don)

LONGEVITY: Perennial

SEASON: Warm

ORIGIN: Native

ECONOMIC VALUE: Wildlife - good   Livestock - poor

The shape of the flower also lends itself to another common name "mexican hat". Upright prairie-coneflower is widely distributed throughout Texas and is considered one of the more common wildflowers. The ray flowers range in color from yellow to red to brown, providing interesting displays.

GROWTH CHARACTERISTICS:

forb, 20-80 cm (8-31 in) tall, branched at the base; flowers in warm seasons with available moisture; reproduces from seeds

DISTINGUISHING CHARACTERISTICS:

Leaves: alternate, simple, 3-12 cm (1 1/4-4 3/4 in) long; blades, pinnately cleft to midrib into 5-11 linear divisions; surfaces strigose to hirsute

Flowers: heads borne singly on a long peduncle; ray flowers yellow or red to brown at the base of petals, drooping; disk flowers brown, columnar, column 1-5 cm (3/8-2 in) long

Fruit: achenes, compressed, about 2 mm (1/16 in) long; pappus 2 tooth-like projections

LIVESTOCK LOSSES:

HABITAT:

prairies and plains. Texas distribution: Areas 1-10

Rudbeckia hirta
blackeyed susan

BLACKEYED SUSAN

Sunflower Family (Asteraceae)

LATIN NAME: *Rudbeckia hirta* L.

LONGEVITY: Perennial

SEASON: Warm

ORIGIN: Native

ECONOMIC VALUE: Wildlife - poor   Livestock - poor

Like many forbs, blackeyed susan produces a basal rosette of leaves the first year and a flowering stalk the second. The Cherokee Indians used a juice extracted from the plant for earache. It is easily grown and readily available from commercial nurseries.

GROWTH CHARACTERISTICS:

forb, 30-90 cm (1-3 ft) tall; flowers May to September; reproduces by seed and rootstock

DISTINGUISHING CHARACTERISTICS:

Leaves: alternate, simple, longer than broad, base subpetiolar to nearly sessile, margins entire to obscurely toothed

Flowers: in heads, solitary at end of a long peduncle; peduncles 4-30 cm (1 1/2-12 in) long; ray flowers 12-20, yellow or orange, 20-35 mm (3/4-1 3/8 in) long; receptacle conical; disk flowers brown

Fruit: achenes, 4-angled in cross section, sides flat to convex

Other: stems, leaves, and calyx hirsute to hispid

LIVESTOCK LOSSES:

HABITAT:

dry plains and prairies; disturbed sites. Texas distribution: Areas 1-9

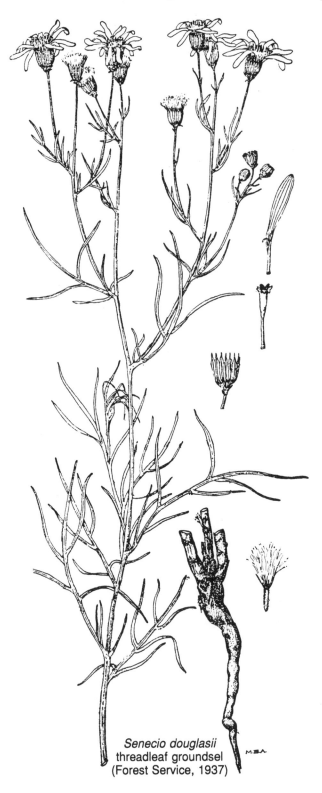

Senecio douglasii
threadleaf groundsel
(Forest Service, 1937)

THREADLEAF GROUNDSEL

Sunflower Family (Asteraceae)

LATIN NAME: *Senecio douglasii* DC.
                         (*Senecio longilobus* Benth.)

LONGEVITY: Perennial

SEASON: Warm

ORIGIN: Native

ECONOMIC VALUE: Wildlife - poor   Livestock - poor (poisonous)

The genus name "Senecio" is from the Latin "senes" which means "old man". It was thus named because of the appearance of stringy leaves, hairy seeds and bald receptacle. A bath with the leaves of threadleaf groundsel is said to relieve arthritic pain.

GROWTH CHARACTERISTICS:

suffrutescent shrub, 30-110 cm (1-3 1/2 ft) tall, plant much branched above and leafy throughout; seed germinates in early spring, flowers May to June; reproduces by seeds

DISTINGUISHING CHARACTERISTICS:

Leaves: simple, alternate, divided into 5-9 filiform divisions; margins rolled inward, tomentose

Flowers: heads in corymbs, lemon yellow; 9-16 mm (11/32-5/8 in) high; phyllary bracts in a single series, brown at the apex

Fruit: achenes, pubescent; pappus of capillary bristles

Other: stem tomentose

LIVESTOCK LOSSES:

poisonous to cattle, sheep, and horses; contains the alkaloid longilobine

HABITAT:

dry plains, grasslands. Texas distribution: Areas 7-10

Silphium laciniatum
compass plant

COMPASS PLANT

Sunflower Family (Asteraceae)

LATIN NAME: *Silphium laciniatum* L.

LONGEVITY: Perennial

SEASON: Warm

ORIGIN: Native

ECONOMIC VALUE: Wildlife - poor   Livestock - good

An unusual characteristic of compass plant is that the ray flowers produce the seed, the disc flowers do not. The opposite is true of most members of the Sunflower family. The name "compass plant" refers to the north-south orientation of the leaves.

GROWTH CHARACTERISTICS:

forb; stems 1-3 m (3-11 ft) tall, stout, striate, scabrous to hispid; reproduces by seeds and a woody taproot

DISTINGUISHING CHARACTERISTICS:

Leaves: alternate, simple, rigid, pinnatifid; basal leaves petiolate, to 40 cm (16 in) long

Flowers: heads arranged in a racemose form; involucres rigid, 2-4 cm (3/4-1 1/2 in) tall; ray flowers yellow, 25-45 mm (1-1 3/4 in) long, fertile; disk flowers yellow, infertile, corolla 5-lobed

Fruit: achenes with dilated wings, glabrous; apical notch 1-3 mm (1/32-1/8 in) deep

LIVESTOCK LOSSES:

HABITAT:

prairies, barren limestone soils. Texas distribution: Areas 1, 4, 5

Vernonia baldwinii
ironweed

IRONWEED

Sunflower Family (Asteraceae)

LATIN NAME: *Vernonia baldwinii* Torr.

LONGEVITY: Perennial

SEASON: Warm

ORIGIN: Native

ECONOMIC VALUE: Wildlife - poor   Livestock - poor

The common name of this plant relates to the toughness of the stem. The plant is extremely difficult to pull out of the ground. The genus name "Vernonia" is after William Vernon, an English botanist who did field work in North America. Various medicinal uses have been made of the roots of ironweed.

GROWTH CHARACTERISTICS:

forb; stems 50-180 cm (20-71 in) tall, seldom branched at the base, much branched at the apex, pubescent; reproduces from seeds

DISTINGUISHING CHARACTERISTICS:

Leaves: alternate, simple, numerous, firm to membranous; blades elliptical to lanceolate, 10-20 cm (4-8 in) long, 2-5 cm (3/4-2 in) wide, serrate, acuminate, glabrous to scabrous above, glabrous to tomentose below with resinous dots

Flowers: in heads; corymbiform arrangement of heads; phyllaries in several series, imbricate; head with 20-40 flowers; ray flowers absent; disk flowers purple, mauve, or rose colored; pappus of coarse bristles in a double series

Fruit: achenes, to 3.5 mm (about 1/8 in) long, ribs 6-10 with droplets of resin, glabrous to pubescent, light brown

Other: upper stem distinctly tomentose in var. *baldwinii*

LIVESTOCK LOSSES:

HABITAT:

upland plains, prairies, open woods, roadsides, and river bottoms. Texas distribution: Areas 1-5, 7-9

Wedelia hispida
orange zexmenia

ORANGE ZEXMENIA

Sunflower Family (Asteraceae)

LATIN NAME: *Wedelia hispida* H.B.K.
                       (*Zexmenia hispida* (H.B.K.) Gray)

LONGEVITY: Perennial

SEASON: Warm

ORIGIN: Native

ECONOMIC VALUE: Wildlife - poor   Livestock - good

The unusual common name "zexmenia" is derived from the previous Latin name. Also known as "orange daisy", the plant thrives equally well under dry or moist conditions. Common along roadsides, it can be transplanted or grown from seed.

GROWTH CHARACTERISTICS:

      small shrub, 40-100 cm (16-39 in) tall, hispid throughout; reproduces by seeds

DISTINGUISHING CHARACTERISTICS:

Leaves: simple, mostly opposite, short petiolate or sessile; blades lanceolate, hispid, base and apex acute

Flowers: in heads, either single or in cymes; heads about 1 cm (3/8 in) wide, phyllaries 2-3 series; ray flowers usually 8, yellow-orange; disk flowers yellow to orange, pappus of 2-3 awns

Fruit: achenes of ray flowers 3-angled; achenes of disk flowers 2-winged

LIVESTOCK LOSSES:

      none

HABITAT:

      rocky hillsides and plateaus. Texas distribution: Areas 2, 6, 7

Opuntia lindheimeri
Texas prickly pear cactus

TEXAS PRICKLY PEAR CACTUS

Cactus Family (Cactaceae)

LATIN NAME: *Opuntia lindheimeri* Engelm.

LONGEVITY: Perennial

SEASON: Warm

ORIGIN: Native

ECONOMIC VALUE: Wildlife - poor   Livestock - poor

Indian and Mexican peoples have long used the fruit and pads of the prickly pear as food. It is becoming popular in trendy restaurants as well as finding a place in the produce departments of many grocery stores. The fruits make delicious jelly. Many species of wildlife utilize prickly pear, including deer and rabbits. Cattle will graze the plant if the spines have been burned off. Reportedly used by 44 kinds of animals for food.

GROWTH CHARACTERISTICS:

shrub with fleshy stems, large, erect to ascending, to 1 m (3 ft) tall; stem segments (pads) flattened, circular to obovate, 10-25 cm (4-10 in) or more long, green; areole with 1-6 spines; spines straight, yellowish, usually less than 4 cm (1 1/2 in) long; glochids yellow to brown, 2-5 mm (1/16-3/16 in) long; reproduces from seeds and pieces of pads (stems)

DISTINGUISHING CHARACTERISTICS:

Leaves: subulate, fleshy, green, early deciduous; found in early spring

Flowers: showy; sepals numerous, intergrading into the numerous petals; petals 5-8 cm (2-3 1/8 in) long, yellow to greenish; stamens numerous from the hypanthium

Fruit: berry, fleshy, 3-7 cm (1 1/4-2 3/4 in) long, purple at maturity; seeds 3-4 mm (1/8-5/32 in) long, tan

LIVESTOCK LOSSES:

HABITAT:

gravelly, rocky, or loamy soils of prairies and savannahs. Texas distribution: Areas 1-7, 10

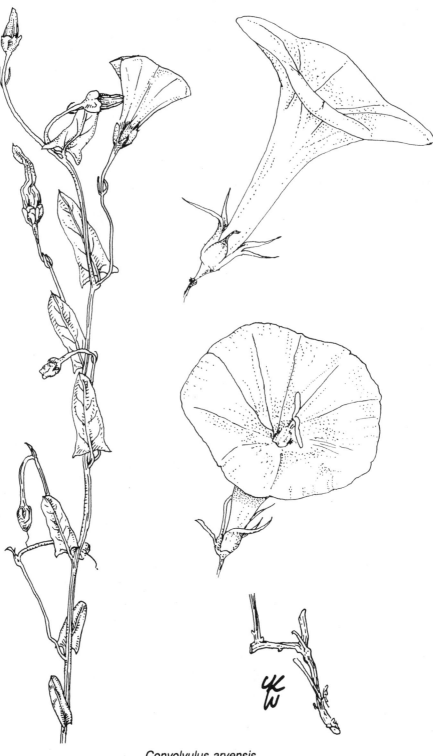

Convolvulus arvensis
field bindweed

FIELD BINDWEED

Morning Glory Family (Convolvulaceae)

LATIN NAME: *Convolvulus arvensis* L.

LONGEVITY: Perennial

SEASON: Warm

ORIGIN: Introduced

ECONOMIC VALUE: Wildlife - poor   Livestock - fair

Field bindweed is also known as "morning glory" for the characteristic of the flowers to remain open in the morning only and "possession vine" for it's ability to "take over" and retain it's place in a habitat.

GROWTH CHARACTERISTICS:

forb; stems to 2 m (6 ft) long, trailing or climbing, twining, usually glabrous; reproduces by seeds

DISTINGUISHING CHARACTERISTICS:

Leaves: alternate, simple; stipules absent; petiole equal to blade length or shorter; blades 1-7 cm (3/8-2 3/4 in) long, 5-35 mm (3/16-1 3/8 in) wide, base frequently cordate, apex acute to acuminate

Flowers: solitary in leaf axils, peduncle shorter than leaf; calyx of 5 united sepals; corolla funnelform, 5 united petals, white, pink, or lavender-pink

Fruit: capsule with 2-4 seeds

LIVESTOCK LOSSES:

HABITAT:

disturbed sites, fields, roadsides, railroad right-of-ways, and gardens. Texas distribution: Areas 2, 4, 5, 7-10

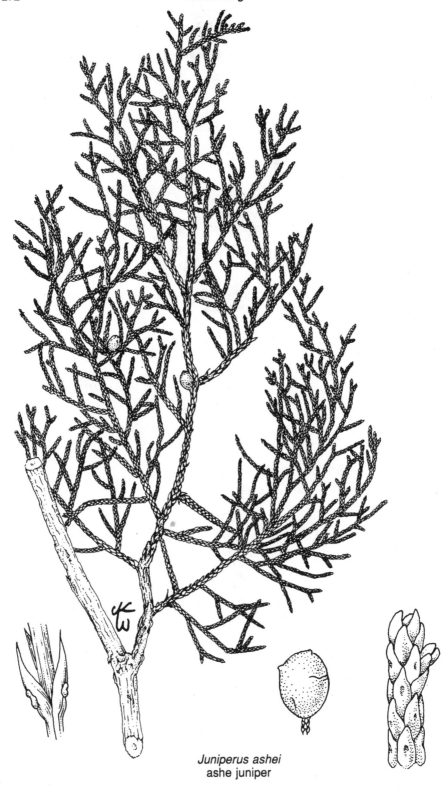

Juniperus ashei
ashe juniper

ASHE JUNIPER

Cypress Family (Cupressaceae)

LATIN NAME: *Juniperus ashei* Buchh.

LONGEVITY: Perennial

SEASON: Cool-Warm (Evergreen)

ORIGIN: Native

ECONOMIC VALUE: Wildlife - fair   Livestock - poor

Ashe juniper is the most common of the junipers in central Texas. The wood is utilized for poles, posts, and fuel. Small mammals and birds use the fruits as food. Whitetail deer will browse Ashe juniper, but it is not a perferred food species. Mature stands of Ashe juniper are necessary for nesting habitat for the endangered golden cheeked warbler.

GROWTH CHARACTERISTICS:

dioecious tree or shrub; 1-6 m (3-20 ft) tall, multiple stems, crown broadly globular or irregular; branches spreading, recurved; twigs gray with age; reproduces by seeds

DISTINGUISHING CHARACTERISTICS:

Leaves: opposite (rarely whorls of 3), aromatic, evergreen, scale-like, appressed, triangular to ovate, 1-2 mm (1/32-1/16 in) long, dark gray-green, swollen gland on back of some leaves

Flowers: small, staminate cones with about 12 scarious scales; ovulate flowers subglobose, of 2-3 series of scales

Fruit: berry-like, globose, 7-9 mm (1/4-11/32 in) long, glaucous, dark-blue; seeds 1-2 per fruit, 5-6 mm (3/16-1/4 in) long, light yellow brown to chocolate brown

Other: bark ashy-gray, thin; sapwood white, heartwood pale brown

LIVESTOCK LOSSES:

HABITAT:

rocky soils of hills, canyons, flats, rimrocks, and breaks. Texas distribution: Areas 5-10

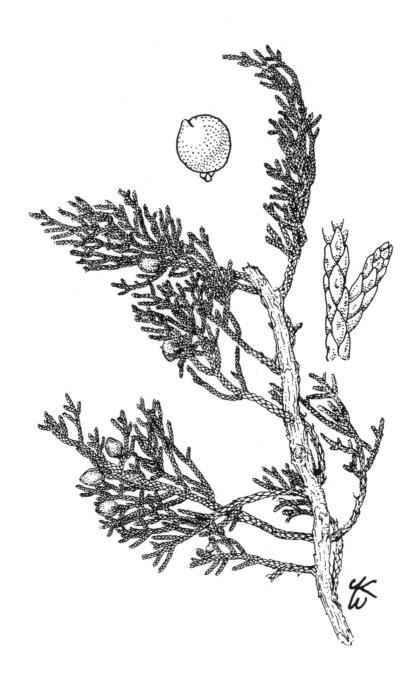

Juniperus pinchotii
redberry juniper

REDBERRY JUNIPER

Cypress Family (Cupressaceae)

LATIN NAME: *Juniperus pinchotii* Sudw.

LONGEVITY: Perennial

SEASON: Cool-Warm (Evergreen)

ORIGIN: Native

ECONOMIC VALUE: Wildlife - poor   Livestock - poor

Redberry juniper is the most common juniper to occur in West Texas and the Panhandle. It is very hardy, and will root sprout when damaged by fire. Oils in all the junipers make them very volatile, almost seeming to explode, when in the path of wildfire.

GROWTH CHARACTERISTICS:

dioecious (rarely monoecious) tree or shrub, 1-6 m (3-20 ft) tall, multiple stems; sprouts readily from stumps; reproduces by seeds and sprouting

DISTINGUISHING CHARACTERISTICS:

Leaves: opposite or in whorls of 3, aromatic, evergreen, scale-like or awl-shaped, appressed, triangular to ovate, acute, 1.4-2.6 mm (1/32-1/8 in) long, with a less obvious gland on the back, yellow green

Flowers: small, staminate cones clustered or single; ovulate cones in 2-3 series of scales

Fruit: berry-like, subglobose, diameter 4-6 mm (5/32-1/4 in); seeds 1-2 per fruit, to 5 mm (3/16 in) long, shiny, chestnut-brown

Other: bark ash-gray, thin; branches with slender erect apicies; wood white in sapwood, light brown to reddish heartwood

LIVESTOCK LOSSES:

HABITAT:

gravelly, rocky soils, usually dry hill to open flats, arroyos; common on gypsum and limestone soils. Texas distribution: Areas 5-10

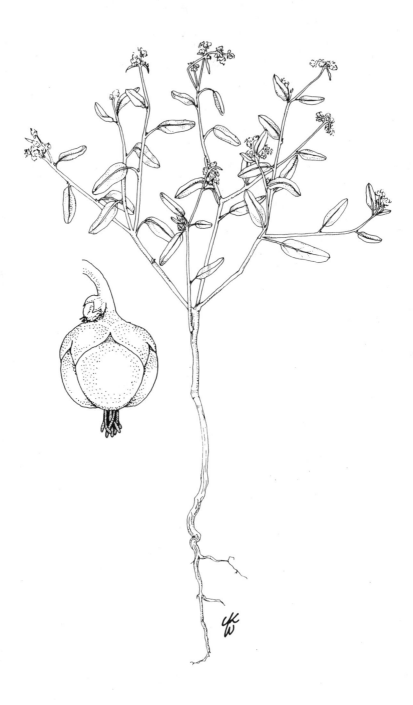

Croton texensis
Texas croton

TEXAS CROTON

Spurge Family (Euphorbiaceae)

LATIN NAME: *Croton texensis* (Klotzch) Muell. Arg.

LONGEVITY: Annual

SEASON: Warm

ORIGIN: Native

ECONOMIC VALUE: Wildlife - good   Livestock - poor

The seeds of Texas croton are a food source for quail and other wild birds. Hopi Indians and early pioneers used the plant medicinally. Oil from the seeds is highly toxic.

GROWTH CHARACTERISTICS:

dioecious forb; stems 20-80 cm (8-31 in) tall, much branched, dense stellate pubescence; reproduces from seeds

DISTINGUISHING CHARACTERISTICS:

Leaves: alternate, simple, short petiolate; blades 2-6 cm (3/4-2 3/8 in) long, linear to oblong, apex acute or rounded, base obtuse or rounded

Flowers: staminate flowers in racemes, calyx with 5 triangular lobes, petal absent; pistillate flowers in racemes, calyx with 5 triangular lobes; petals absent, styles 3

Fruit: capsule, 4-6 mm (5/32-1/4 in) long, globose to ovoid, hairs stellate; seeds 3-4 mm (1/8-5/32 in) long

LIVESTOCK LOSSES:

HABITAT:

a weed of disturbed sites, sandy to sandy loam soils, old fields are sometimes disked to increase the croton as dove food. Texas distribution: Areas 2-10

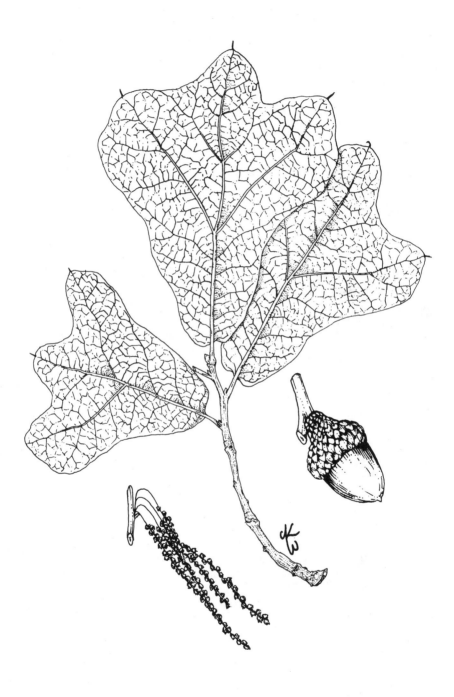

Quercus marilandica
blackjack oak

BLACKJACK OAK

Beech Family (Fagaceae)

LATIN NAME: *Quercus marilandica* Muench.

LONGEVITY: Perennial

SEASON: Warm

ORIGIN: Native

ECONOMIC VALUE: Wildlife - good   Livestock - good (poisonous)

Sometimes growing in colonies, blackjack oak wood is used for fence posts, fuel, and charcoal. The acorns provide food for both whitetail deer and turkey.

GROWTH CHARACTERISTICS:

monoecious tree or shrub, to 12 m (40 ft) tall, deciduous, flowers in April; reproduces by seeds and sprouts

DISTINGUISHING CHARACTERISTICS:

Leaves: alternate, simple; blades 10-22 cm (4-8 3/4 in) long, 8-17 cm (3 1/8-6 3/4 in) wide, broadly obovate, margins revolute, apex 3-lobed; nerves or midvein of lobes extend into a bristle; upper surface dark green, lower surface dull

Flowers: unisexual in staminate and pistillate catkins

Fruit: acorns, cap or cup enclosing 1/3 to 1/2 their length; nut oblong, ripens in two years

Other: bark dark brown or black, deeply fissured

LIVESTOCK LOSSES:

tannic acid poisoning can occur with cattle; see *Quercus virginiana* for symptoms

HABITAT:

dry, sandy, and sterile soils. Texas distribution: Areas 1-3, 7, 8

Quercus stellata
post oak

POST OAK

Beech Family (Fagaceae)

LATIN NAME: *Quercus stellata* Wang.

LONGEVITY: Perennial

SEASON: Warm

ORIGIN: Native

ECONOMIC VALUE: Wildlife - fair   Livestock - poor (poisonous)

Post oak is the dominant member of the Post Oak Savannah and the Cross-timbers vegetative areas of Texas. It has been cultivated since 1819. The species name "stellata" refers to the hairs on the leaves that appear star shaped from above.

GROWTH CHARACTERISTICS:

monoecious tree or shrub, 10-25 m (32-82 ft) tall, deciduous, starts growth in March to April with the appearance of the inflorescence; leaves follow flowers; fruit matures September to October; reproduces by seeds and sprouts

DISTINGUISHING CHARACTERISTICS:

Leaves: alternate, simple; blades 10-15 cm (4-6 in) long, 7-10 cm (2 3/4-4 in) wide, leathery, broadest above the middle with 3-5 short to deep lobes; apex rounded; base-wedge shaped; stellate hairs on the lower surface

Flowers: unisexual in staminate or pistillate catkins

Fruit: acorns occur in clusters of 2 to 4, cup or cap is top-shaped and covers one-third of the nut

Other: bark dark gray with rough, scaly ridges

LIVESTOCK LOSSES:

tannic acid poisoning may be a problem for cattle; see *Quercus virginiana* for symptoms

HABITAT:

rocky and sandy ridges. Texas distribution: Areas 1-8

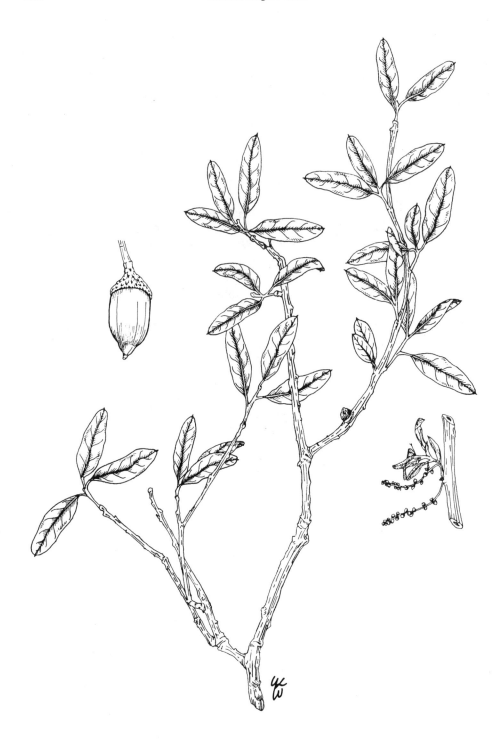

Quercus virginiana
live oak

LIVE OAK

Beech Family (Fagaceae)

LATIN NAME: *Quercus virginiana* Mill.

LONGEVITY: Perennial

SEASON: Cool-Warm (Evergreen)

ORIGIN: Native

ECONOMIC VALUE: Wildlife - good   Livestock - fair (poisonous)

Also known as "encino" among the Spanish speaking peoples, live oak is a highly prized ornamental. Early Indians used an oil made from the acorns for cooking purposes.

GROWTH CHARACTERISTICS:

monoecious trees, 3-10 m (9-32 ft) tall, crown spreading; bark deeply furrowed, dark brownish black, youngest twigs gray; reproduces by seeds

DISTINGUISHING CHARACTERISTICS:

Leaves: alternate, simple; petioles 3-9 mm (1/8-11/32 in) long; blades thick, 2-11 cm (3/4-4 3/8 in) long, 1-5 cm (3/8-2 in) wide, obovate, oblanceolate to elliptic; apices acute to rounded; bases rounded to cuneate; margins entire, toothed or lobed, revolute; upper surface shiny, glabrous; lower surface with dense stellate hairs

Flowers: unisexual; staminate catkins 2-4 cm (3/4-1 1/2 in) long, densely flowered, anthers pubescent; pistillate catkins to 20 mm (3/4 in) long, 1-several flowered

Fruit: acorn, matures in 1 year, peduncle 5-40 mm (3/16-1 1/2 in) long; cup to 10 mm (3/8 in) high, diameter to 15 mm (9/16 in) wide; acorn 15-35 mm (9/16-1 3/8 in) long, glabrous, shiny brown

LIVESTOCK LOSSES:

gallic and tannic acids are toxic compounds in some oak species, these acids affect cattle, sheep and goats with emaciation, edema, mucous and/or blood in the feces

HABITAT:

upland sites, rocky soils. Texas distribution: Areas 2-3, 5-8

Krameria lanceolata
trailing ratany

TRAILING RATANY

Ratany Family (Krameriaceae)

LATIN NAME: *Krameria lanceolata* Torr.

LONGEVITY: Perennial

SEASON: Warm

ORIGIN: Native

ECONOMIC VALUE: Wildlife - fair   Livestock - fair

Trailing ratany is pollinated by only the female bees of the genus "Centris". While most flowers offer nectar of bees, trailing ratany provides oil which the bees mix with pollen. They then use this oil-pollen mixture to provide food for their larvae. Trailing ratany is also valuable as forage for whitetail deer.

GROWTH CHARACTERISTICS:

forb; stems 0.1-1.8 m (4-79 in) long, prostrate or trailing, sometimes supported by other vegetation, gray pubescence; rootstocks woody; reproduces by seeds

DISTINGUISHING CHARACTERISTICS:

Leaves: alternate, simple; stipules absent; linear or occasionally oblong, 6-22 mm (1/4-13/16 in) long

Flowers: single, axillary; sepals 4-5, unequal; petals 5, unequal, reddish-purple; stamens 4

Fruit: indehiscent pod, globose, woolly, diameter 5-8 mm (3/16-5/16 in); armed with prickles to 4 mm (5/32 in) long

Other: stipules absent

LIVESTOCK LOSSES:

HABITAT:

widespread; absent in wet sites. Texas distribution: Areas 2-10

Monarda citriodora
beebalm

BEEBALM

Mint Family (Lamiaceae)

LATIN NAME: *Monarda citriodora* Cerv.

LONGEVITY: Annual

SEASON: Warm

ORIGIN: Native

ECONOMIC VALUE: Wildlife - poor   Livestock - poor

Beebalm is also known as "lemon mint". The Latin name "citriodora" refers to this lemon odor. The genus "Monarda" honors Nicolas Monardes, an early Spanish writer who studied medicinal plants. Beebalm reportedly makes a fair insect repellent when crushed and rubbed on the skin. The commercially available citronella insect repellent is derived from a compound within beebalm. May be heavily utilized by whitetail deer.

GROWTH CHARACTERISTICS:

aromatic forb; stems 15-90 cm (6-35 in) tall, branching in the inflorescences; curly pubescence; reproduces by seeds

DISTINGUISHING CHARACTERISTICS:

Leaves: opposite, simple; petioles to 3 mm (1/8 in) long; blades lanceolate to oblong, longest 3-6 cm (1 1/4-2 3/8 in) long, dotted with minute oil glands, puberulent to glabrate, margins nearly entire

Flowers: in verticils; outer bracts leaf-like, spreading or reflexed; inner bracts 5-8 mm (3/16-5/16 in) long, oblong to lanceolate, acuminate; calyx tube 6-13 mm (1/4-1/2 in) long, hirsute, aristate teeth 2-7 mm (1/16-1/4 in) long; corolla white or pink with purple dots, tube 7-18 mm (1/4-11/16 in) long, zygomorphic, 2-lipped

Fruit: nutlets, in a group of 4 with 1 seed each, 1.5-2 mm (about 1/16 in) long, yellow brown

Other: stems square; aromatic

LIVESTOCK LOSSES:

HABITAT:

roadsides, prairies, meadows, and savannahs on sandy loams to rocky loam throughout Texas. Texas distribution: Areas 1-10

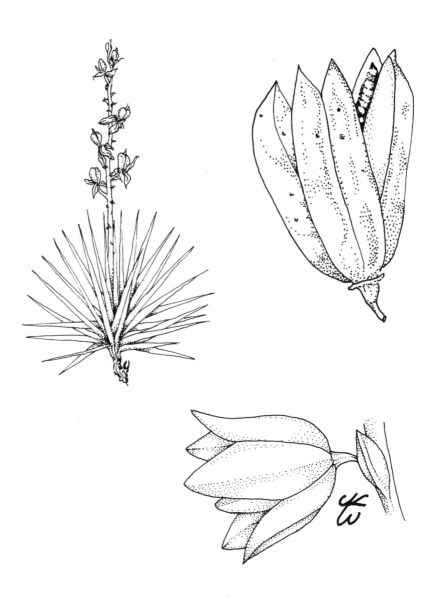

Yucca constricta
buckley yucca

BUCKLEY YUCCA

Lily Family (Liliaceae)

LATIN NAME: *Yucca constricta* (Trel.) McKelvey

LONGEVITY: Perennial

SEASON: Warm

ORIGIN: Native

ECONOMIC VALUE: Wildlife - poor   Livestock - poor

While many species of yuccas have trunks, Buckley yucca does not. Yuccas have been used by both native peoples and early settlers of the Southwest for baskets, mats, sandals, and rope. The flowers may be eaten raw and the dried pods have been roasted and made into flour. Yucca provides an important source of food for jack rabbits when other green forage is not available. Hummingbirds utilize the flower.

GROWTH CHARACTERISTICS:

forb without a stem or with short stems to 40 cm (16 in) tall; clump forming with numerous heads of leaves; reproduces by seeds

DISTINGUISHING CHARACTERISTICS:

Leaves: in heads; blades 30-60 cm (1-2 ft) long, 5-12 mm (3/16-1/2 in) wide, linear, nearly flat, striate; margins green or white, becoming fibrous along the margins

Flowers: flowering stalk 1-3 m (3-11 ft) tall; flowers in panicles, 40-110 cm (16-43 in) long, diameter to 70 cm (28 in) wide; flowers greenish white, 6 tepals in 2 series; sepals 30-45 mm (1 1/4-1 3/4 in) long; petals 40-50 mm (1 1/2-1 3/4 in) long; stamens 6; stigmas 3

Fruit: capsule, 45-65 cm (1 3/4-2 1/2 in) long, oblong, mucronate; seed to 18 mm (11/16 in) wide, black, winged, shiny

Other: important for jack rabbits; cattle utilize the flowers and stalk; deer use the fruit

LIVESTOCK LOSSES:

HABITAT:

grasslands, savannahs, and brushland. Texas distribution: Areas 2, 5-9

Zigadenus nuttallii
nuttall deathcamas

NUTTALL DEATHCAMAS

Lily Family (Liliaceae)

LATIN NAME: *Zigadenus nuttallii* (Gray) S. Wats.

LONGEVITY: Perennial

SEASON: Cool

ORIGIN: Native

ECONOMIC VALUE: Wildlife - poor   Livestock - poor (poisonous)

Nuttall deathcamas is also very toxic to humans and livestock causing vomiting, breathing difficulty, coma, and possibly even death. The plants grow in some of the same habitats as wild onions (Allium spp.). Care must be taken not to confuse the two plants as the onion is edible. The pollen and nectar are not toxic to insects, as a variety of insects utilize them. The plant is named for Thomas Nuttall, botanical collector.

GROWTH CHARACTERISTICS:

forb; stem 30-70 cm (1-2 1/2 ft) tall from a bulb; bulb thin coated, not fibrous, several cm below the soil surface; reproduces by seeds

DISTINGUISHING CHARACTERISTICS:

Leaves: mainly basal; blades linear, flat to folded, 30-58 cm (1-2 ft) long, 8-18 mm (5/16-11/16 in) wide, sheathing stem, curved

Flowers: raceme inflorescence; pedicels 5-28 mm (3/16-1 1/8 in) long, ascending to spreading, subtended by linear bracts; flowers of 6 sepals, creamy white to yellow; stamens 6; style 3-parted

Fruit: capsule, 7-14 mm (1/4-9/16 in) long, many seeded; seeds 1.4-2.2 mm (about 1/16 in) long

LIVESTOCK LOSSES:

toxic principle is an alkaloid; poisonous to cattle, sheep, and horses; all parts toxic even when dry; symptoms include salivation, nausea, low temperature, weak and irregular pulse, difficult breathing, coma, death

HABITAT:

prairies, savannahs; often in rocky sites. Texas distribution: Areas 1, 3-5, 7

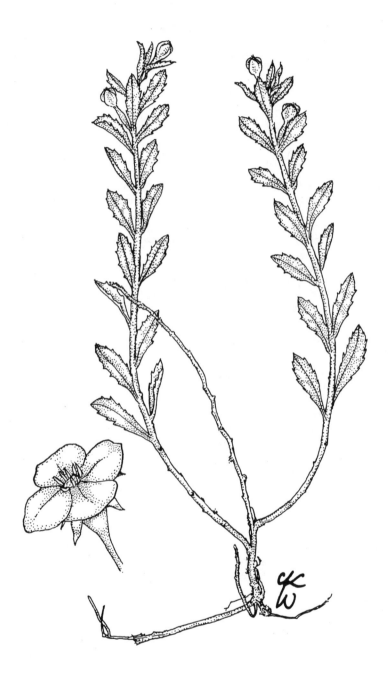

Calylophus serrulatus
halfshrub sundrop

HALFSHRUB SUNDROP

Evening Primrose Family (Onagraceae)

LATIN NAME: *Calylophus serrulatus* (Nutt.) Raven
(*Oenothera serrulata* Nutt.)

LONGEVITY: Perennial

SEASON: Warm

ORIGIN: Native

ECONOMIC VALUE: Wildlife - fair   Livestock - good

Flowers of halfshrub sundrop open at sunrise, lending the common name. It is also known as "wire primrose". Sometimes used as an ornamental, the plant is easily propagated by root divisions. Early medicinal uses included treating ailments of the eye and sore throats.

GROWTH CHARACTERISTICS:

suffrutescent shrub (herbaceous above, woody below), 5-80 cm (2-31 in) tall; reproduces by seeds

DISTINGUISHING CHARACTERISTICS:

Leaves: alternate, simple; stipules absent; linear to oblanceolate, 1-7 cm (3/8-2 3/4 in) long, 2-7 mm (1/16-1/4 in) wide, glabrous to canescent, margins denticulate

Flowers: calyx 4-parted; 3-7 mm (1/8-1/4 in) long, distinct, apex free; corolla 4-parted, petals 6-12 mm (1/4-1/2 in) long, yellow; stamens 8; stigma 4-lobed

Fruit: capsule, 10-30 mm (3/8-1 1/4 in) long, thick-walled with 2 rows of seeds per locule; seeds 1-2 mm (1/32-1/16 in) long, apex truncate

LIVESTOCK LOSSES:

HABITAT:

hillsides, valleys, open woodlands, and roadsides in open rocky or sandy areas of the Panhandle. Texas distribution: Areas 2-9

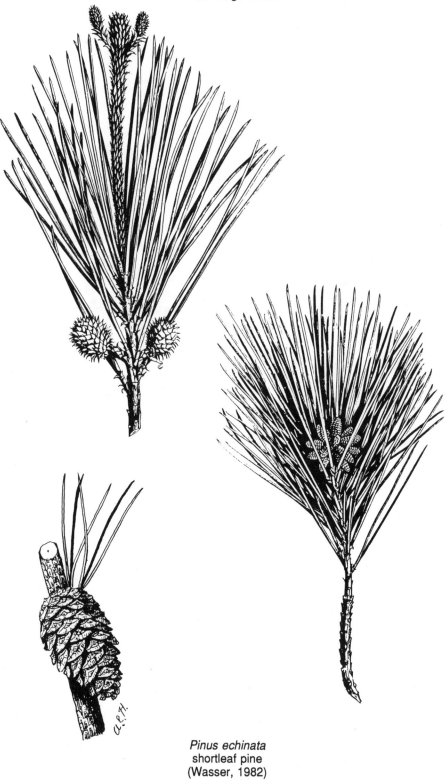

Pinus echinata
shortleaf pine
(Wasser, 1982)

SHORTLEAF PINE

Pine Family (Pinaceae)

LATIN NAME: *Pinus echinata* Mill.

LONGEVITY: Perennial

SEASON: Cool-Warm (Evergreen)

ORIGIN: Native

ECONOMIC VALUE: Wildlife - poor   Livestock - poor

Wood of the shortleaf pine is used for general construction purposes and for lower grade furniture. It is an important species to the Texas lumber industry. It is also used in reforestation efforts in Texas.

GROWTH CHARACTERISTICS:

monoecious tree; trunk to 35 m (114 ft) tall, diameter 60-90 cm (24-35 in) wide; crown pyramidal; reproduces by seeds

DISTINGUISHING CHARACTERISTICS:

Leaves: needles in fascicles of 2 to 3, 7-13 cm (2 3/4-5 1/8 in) long, flexible, evergreen

Flowers: unisexual; staminate cones yellow-brown to pinkish at the twig apex; ovulate cones solitary or in clusters, pinkish

Fruit: woody cone, 4-7 cm (1 1/2-2 3/4 in) long, scales thin, with a short straight to curved prickle; seeds 7-8 mm (1/4-5/16 in) long, brown, nearly triangular

Other: bark black and rough on young stems

LIVESTOCK LOSSES:

HABITAT:

hills, flatlands and wooded slopes of the eastern part of the State; timber species. Texas distribution: Areas 1-3

Pinus taeda
loblolly pine
(Wasser, 1982)

LOBLOLLY PINE

Pine Family (Pinaceae)

LATIN NAME:	*Pinus taeda* L.
LONGEVITY:	Perennial
SEASON:	Cool-Warm (Evergreen)
ORIGIN:	Native
ECONOMIC VALUE:	Wildlife - poor Livestock - poor

Loblolly pine is a very fast growing tree that has been cultivated since 1713. The "Lost Pines" in Bastrop County are loblolly pines. The species is used for revegetating lignite mines. Cultivated for lumber and pulp. Absolutely essential to the endangered "red-cockaded woodpecker" in East Texas.

GROWTH CHARACTERISTICS:

monoecious tree, to 30 m (100 ft) tall, trunk to 1 m (3 ft) diameter; bark reddish-brown to black when immature, plated with age; seeds mature in September or October; reproduces by seeds

DISTINGUISHING CHARACTERISTICS:

Leaves: needles in fascicles of 3, 15-23 cm (6-9 in) long, pale green, evergreen

Flowers: unisexual; staminate cones yellow, in small cluster near the branch apex; ovulate cones woody 5-15 cm (2-6 in) long, scales with a reflexed spine at the apex

Fruit: woody scaled cones, 6-11 cm (2 3/8-4 3/8 in) long

LIVESTOCK LOSSES:

HABITAT:

adapted to many soils from piedmont to poorly drained. Texas distribution: Areas 1-3

Karwinskia humboldtiana
coyotillo

COYOTILLO

Buckhorn Family (Rhamnaceae)

LATIN NAME: *Karwinskia humboldtiana* (R. & S.) Zucc.

LONGEVITY: Perennial

SEASON: Warm

ORIGIN: Native

ECONOMIC VALUE: Wildlife - poor   Livestock - poor (poisonous)

Oily seeds of coyotillo are very poisonous, causing paralysis of limbs in humans and animals, especially sheep. A concoction of roots and leaves is used to treat fevers in Mexico. The plant is easily propagated by root division.

GROWTH CHARACTERISTICS:

unarmed shrub, 1-2.2 m (3-7 ft) tall, multiple stems, usually glabrous; reproduces by seeds

DISTINGUISHING CHARACTERISTICS:

Leaves: simple, opposite, short petioled; blades 3-8 cm (1 1/4-3 1/8 in) long, oblong to elliptic, apex and base acute to rounded, margins entire to slightly crenate, secondary veins parallel, lower surface light green

Flowers: in few flowered clusters, inflorescence an axillary cyme; petals 5 with 5 stamens positioned opposite the petals

Fruit: drupe, globose, black at maturity

LIVESTOCK LOSSES:

toxic to most livestock; symptoms include weakness, trembling, and respiratory distress; animals that die have pulmonary edema

HABITAT:

dry plains and plateaus. Texas distribution: Areas 2, 6, 7, 10

Ziziphus obtusifolia
lotebush

LOTEBUSH

Buckhorn Family (Rhamnaceae)

LATIN NAME: *Ziziphus obtusifolia* (T. & G.) Gray

LONGEVITY: Perennial

SEASON: Warm

ORIGIN: Native

ECONOMIC VALUE: Wildlife - good   Livestock - poor

Lotebush is also known as "gumdrop tree". The fruits of this shrub are food for a wide variety of birds. Lotebush is perhaps one of the best quail loafing covers.

GROWTH CHARACTERISTICS:

thorned shrub, to 4 m (14 ft) tall, densely branched; reproduces by seeds

DISTINGUISHING CHARACTERISTICS:

Leaves: alternate, simple; blades deltoid to oblong, gray-green; deltoid leaves serrate

Flowers: in axillary cymes; petals present, greenish, early deciduous

Fruit: drupe with 2-celled stone, round to elongated, dark purple

Other: branches gray with a wax-like bloom and a short straight thorn at the end

LIVESTOCK LOSSES:

HABITAT:

locally abundant on dry plains in the drier parts of the State. Texas distribution: Areas 2, 5-8, 10

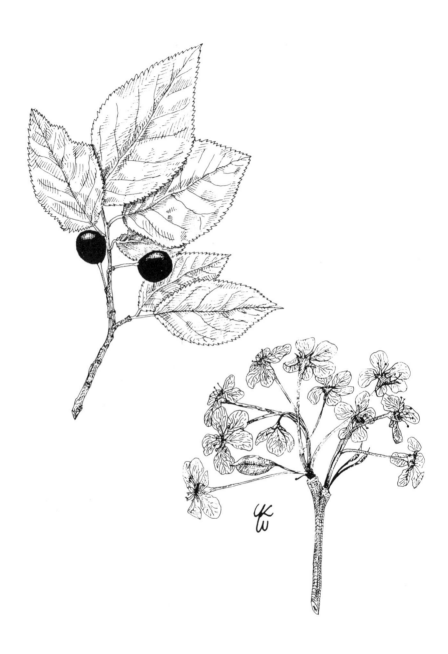

Prunus mexicana
Mexican plum

MEXICAN PLUM

Rose Family (Rosaceae)

LATIN NAME: *Prunus mexicana* Wats.

LONGEVITY: Perennial

SEASON: Cool

ORIGIN: Native

ECONOMIC VALUE: Wildlife - good (birds)   Livestock - poor (poisonous)

Mexican plum does not "sucker" or root sprout to form thickets like other species of plum. It is used by whitetail and mule deer as browse. Deer, foxes, coyotes, racoons, ringtails, and turkey eat the fruits also. The fruits are often gathered and make delicious jams and jellies.

GROWTH CHARACTERISTICS:

tree, to 10 m (33 ft) tall, branchlets glabrous to pubescent; fruiting July to September; reproduces by seeds

DISTINGUISHING CHARACTERISTICS:

Leaves: alternate, simple; petiole glandular; blades 5-14 cm (2-5 1/2 in) long, obovate to oblong, double serrate, acuminate, base subcordate, glabrous above (pubescent when young), pubescent beneath

Flowers: in fascicles of 2-4; sepals 5, lobes dentate, distinct; petals 5, white, distinct

Fruit: drupe, 2-3 cm (3/4-1 1/4 in) long, globose to suborbicular, waxy bloom, purplish-red; stone turgid, obovoid

LIVESTOCK LOSSES:

cattle are most likely to be poisoned, may develop hydrocyanic acid poisoning under conditions of plant stress such as freezing, wilting, and bruising; rapid acting poison with death occuring in 15 minutes to several hours after eating the leaves

HABITAT:

river bottoms, hillsides, and prairies. Texas distribution: Areas 2-5, 7

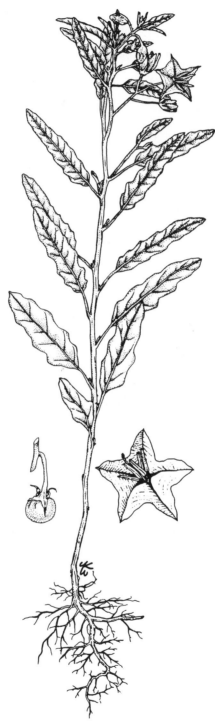

Solanum elaeagnifolium
silverleaf nightshade

SILVERLEAF NIGHTSHADE

Nightshade Family (Solanaceae)

LATIN NAME: *Solanum elaeagnifolium* Cav.

LONGEVITY: Perennial

SEASON: Warm

ORIGIN: Native

ECONOMIC VALUE: Wildlife - poor   Livestock - poor (poisonous)

The genus name comes from the Latin word "solamen" which means "quieting" referring to the narcotic characteristics of the poison. Other names for the plant are "white horsenettle" and "whiteweed". It has been credited for a variety of medicinal uses from treating poison ivy to tooth ailments. The fruits were used by early natives to curdle cheese. The plant is an aggressive sprouter from deep, tough roots. Although known mainly for its poisonous nature, the plant is in the same family as many very valuable plants including chili peppers, tomato, potato, eggplant, and petunia.

GROWTH CHARACTERISTICS:

forb; stems 30-95 cm (1-3 ft) tall, armed with sharp prickles; reproduces by seeds and deep running rootstocks

DISTINGUISHING CHARACTERISTICS:

Leaves: alternate, simple; blades 5-15 cm (2-6 in) long, oblong to linear, sinuate to undulate, apex obtuse to rounded, stellate pubescence silvery white; mature leaves may develop spines along the underside of the midvein

Flowers: inflorescence in axillary cymes; sepals 5, connate; corolla of 5 petals, connate, pale purple to white, apex acute

Fruit: berry, diameter 8-15 mm (5/16-9/16 in), subglobose, yellow to black

LIVESTOCK LOSSES:

toxic to all classes of livestock; glycoalkaloid toxin of fruit may cause poisoning in cattle when fed at 0.1 to 0.3 percent of the animal's body weight; for treatment, place poisoned animal in shade, feed and water regularly

HABITAT:

disturbed sites, most commonly found on limestone derived soils. Texas distribution: Areas 1-10

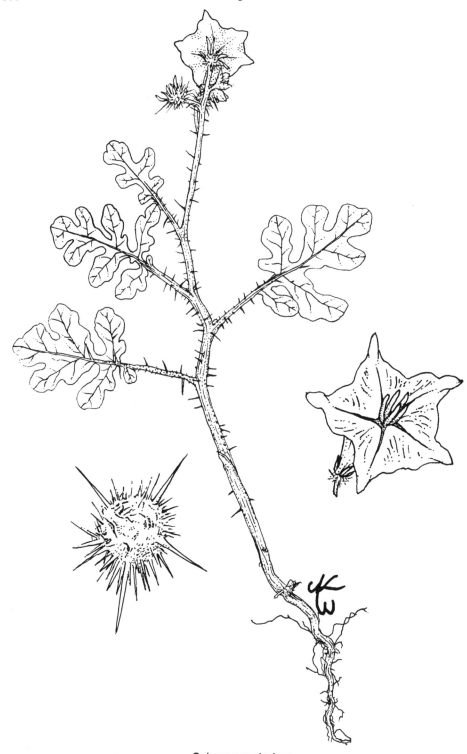

Solanum rostratum
buffaloburr

BUFFALOBURR

Nightshade Family (Solanaceae)

LATIN NAME: *Solanum rostratum* Dun.

LONGEVITY: Annual

SEASON: Warm

ORIGIN: Native

ECONOMIC VALUE: Wildlife - poor   Livestock - poor (poisonous)

Prickles on the buffaloburr plant cause skin irritations to animals and any human willing to handle it. The common name refers to the fact that when the buffalo would wallow in muddy areas with this plant present, the burs would adhere to their hides. Mowing in the early stages of growth is an effective control method for buffaloburr.

GROWTH CHARACTERISTICS:

forb; stems 20-70 cm (8-28 in) tall, pubescence stellate and yellowish, armed with straight prickles; reproduces by seeds

DISTINGUISHING CHARACTERISTICS:

Leaves: alternate, simple, pinnitifid

Flowers: racemes; calyx 5-parted, connate, spiny; corolla 5-parted, connate, yellow, slightly irregular, diameter 18-25 mm (11/16-1 in) wide, stamens 5

Fruit: berry, enclosed by the adhering calyx, many seeded

LIVESTOCK LOSSES:

alkaloid (solanine) poisons horses, cattle, sheep, goats, swine, and man; symptoms include labored breathing, weakness, trembling; dead animals may exhibit only excessive salivation

HABITAT:

weed in disturbed sites such as overgrazed pasture, rangelands, or along roadsides. Texas distribution: Areas 1-10

Aloysia gratissima
whitebrush

WHITEBRUSH

Vervain Family (Verbenaceae)

LATIN NAME: *Aloysia gratissima* (Gill. & Hook.) Troncoso

LONGEVITY: Perennial

SEASON: Warm

ORIGIN: Native

ECONOMIC VALUE: Wildlife - poor   Livestock - poor (poisonous)

Another name for whitebrush is "beebrush", referring to it's use as a honey plant. The flowers have a distinct vanilla aroma and was used in Mexico to treat diseases of the urinary tract. It is easily propogated for horticultural purposes.

GROWTH CHARACTERISTICS:

thicket forming shrub, aromatic, much branched, to 2.5 m (10 ft) tall, twigs gray; flowers whenever sufficient moisture is available; reproduces by seeds

DISTINGUISHING CHARACTERISTICS:

Leaves: opposite, simple, sessile to short petiolate; blades 3-28 mm (1/8-1 1/8 in) long, dull green, apex obtuse to acute, base cuneate, margins entire to serrate, glandular punctate

Flowers: inflorescence a spike or raceme, loosely flowered; calyx campanulate, hirsute, 4-lobed; corolla 3-3.5 mm (about 1/8 in) long, whitish, vanilla odor, zygomorphic

Fruit: schizocarp, small, dry; seeds without endosperm

Other: wood yellow

LIVESTOCK LOSSES:

poisonous principle unknown, water soluble; poisonous to livestock (horses, mules, and burros), symptoms in horses are nervousness and emaciation, weakness followed by death; cumulative poison

HABITAT:

desert grasslands, woods, rocky hillsides, low places, rocky creek-beds, and chaparral thickets. Texas distribution: Areas 2-8, 10

GLOSSARY

A -	Prefix meaning without.
Abaxial	Located on the side away from the axis; dorsal.
Achene	1-seeded, indehiscent dry fruit with a relatively thin wall in which the seed coat is not fused to the ovary wall.
Acorn	A modified nut of the oak tree.
Acuminate	Gradually tapering to a sharp point; point is drawn out.
Acute	Sharply pointed, but less tapering than acuminate; angle 90° or less.
Adaxial	Located on the side nearest the axis; ventral.
Adhere	To stick fast.
Adherent	Sticking or clinging.
Adnate	Fusion of unlike parts (e.g., fusion of palea to the caryopsis in *Bromus*).
Alternate	Located singly at each node. An arrangement of parts (e.g., leaves) placed at different heights along an axis.
Annual	Completing life cycle from seed to maturity to death within 1 year or one season.
Anther	The pollen bearing portion of the stamen.
Antrorse	Directed upward or forward toward the apex.
Apex	Uppermost tip of a structure.
Apices	Plural of apex.
Apical	Located at the tip.
Appressed	Lying against an organ in the direction of the apex.
Areole	A small pit or raised area on the stem of cacti, often bearing tufts of hair, pines, or glochids.
Aristate	Provided with a short awn or bristle from the apex, edge or back of an organ.
Aromatic	Having an odor, fragrant or otherwise; bearing volatile essential oils.
Articulate	Jointed; a node for natural separation of parts.
Ascending	Sloping or rising obliquely upward.
Asymetrical	Not having planes which divide the structure into mirror-image halves.
Attenuate	Gradually narrowing to a pointed apex or base; sharper than acute.
Auricle	A finger-like appendage of flange of tissue at the junction of the blade and sheath in some grasses. Holds the split sheath to the culm.
Awl-shaped	Narrow or sharply pointed, usually small; tapering from a narrow base to a pointed apex.
Awn	A slender bristle at the end or on the back or edge of an organ. The extension of the nerve (vein) of spikelet bracts beyond the leaf-like tissue.
Axil	The upper angle between an organ (branch) and its axis.
Axillary	Occurring in an axil.
Axis	The central stem of an inflorescence, particularly of a panicle.
Barbed	Retrorse projections or hairs.
Basal	Referring to the base or located there; the lower portion of a structure.
Bearded	Bearing long, stiff hairs.
Berry	A fleshy indehiscent fruit with multiple ovules, such as a tomato.
Bi-	Two.

Bifid	Apex with one cleft or having two teeth.
Bilateral	Two sided; structures on two sides of an organ.
Bipinnate	Twice pinnately compound.
Bisexual	Having both sexes; a hermaphrodite.
Blade	The part of the leaf above the sheath.
Bloom	A waxy covering on surfaces, such as fruits and leaves; usually results in a bluish color.
Bract	A modified leaf (e.g., glumes, lemmas, paleas).
Branch	A lateral stem; part of the panicle inflorescence.
Branchlet	A very small branch.
Bristle	A stiff, slender hair or appendage likened to a hog's bristle.
Bud	An undeveloped stem, branch, leaf, or flower.
Bulb	A subterranean bud with fleshy scales, such as those of an onion.
Bur	A rough or prickly covering surrounding the fruits or spikelets of some genera.
Caespitose	Tufted; several or many stems in a close tuft.
Callus	The indurate downward extension of the mature lemma in *Stipa*, *Aristida*, and some other genera.
Calyx	Sepals of a flower considered collectively; usually green bracts that subtend the petals.
Campanulate	Shaped like a bell.
Canescent	Gray or pale colored because of a dense pubescence.
Cap	A cup-like structure made of involucral bracts that subtend the acorn.
Capillary	Very slender or hairlike.
Capitate	In a globular cluster or head.
Capsule	Dry, dehiscent fruit of more than 1 carpel with more than two seeds.
Carpel	The ovule bearing structure of a flower.
Caryopsis	The fruit or grain of grasses. A dry, indehiscent, one-seeded fruit in which the pericarp is adnate to ovary wall (seed coat).
Catkin	Dense spike or raceme with many small, usually naked, flowers; an ament such as in willows or aspen.
Caudate	Having a caudex.
Caudex	Short, usually woody, vertical stem located below the soil surface; new shoots arise from the caudex each year.
Cauline	Belonging to the stem, such as cauline leaves.
Central axis	The main axis of the inflorescence.
Central groove	A longitudinal depression in the sides of the pedicels of *Bothriochloa*.
Chaffy	A condition of a head inflorescence in the Asteraceae where individual flowers are subtended by a thin, dry bract.
Ciliate	Fringed with hairs on the margin.
Cleft	A division or cut half-way to the base or midrib.
Cleistogamous	Applied to flowers or florets fertilized without opening.
Collar	The area on the outer (adaxial) side of the leaf at the junction of the sheath and blade.
Column	The lower, undivided part of the awns of certain *Aristida* species.
Coma	Tuft of hair (e.g., on the milkweed seed).

Compound	Having two or more similar parts in one organ (e.g., a compound leaf or a compound pistil).
Compressed	Flattened strongly, typically laterally; keeled.
Concave	Dished inward, an existing hollow.
Cones	Cluster of scales on an axis, scales may be persistent or deciduous.
Conical	Cone-shaped.
Connate	Fusion of like parts (e.g., petals to form a corolla tube).
Continuous	The rachis or other organ that does not disarticulate (e.g., the inflorescence of *Elytrigia*).
Contracted	Narrow or dense inflorescences, the branches being short or appressed.
Convex	Rounded on the surface.
Cordate	The heart-shaped base and pointed tip of a structure (e.g., a leaf blade).
Corm	Short, bulb-like stem.
Corolla	Composed of petals; collectively the petals, usually white or brightly colored.
Corymb	A simple racemose inflorescence that is flat-topped; an indeterminate inflorescence.
Corymbiform	Having the form of a corymb.
Corymbose	Arranged in a corymb.
Crenate	Scalloped margins; rounded teeth.
Crisp	Undulating in the horizontal plane (crinkled).
Crown	The persistent base of a perennial; the canopy of a tree.
Culm	The jointed grass stem, composed of nodes, internodes, leaves, and axillary buds.
Cuneate	Wedge-shaped; narrow at point of attachment.
Cup	A cup or cap-like structure made of involucral bracts that subtends the acorn.
Cylindrical	Shaped like a tube, round in cross section with parallel margins.
Cyme	A convex or flat-topped flower cluster with the central flower the first to open; inflorescence is determinate.
Deciduous	Not persisting, falling away in less than one year.
Decumbent	Curved upward from a horizontal or inclined base.
Deflexed	Turned downward abruptly.
Dehiscent	Opening at maturity along a definite suture.
Deltoid	Triangular in outline; shaped like the Greek letter delta.
Dense	Inflorescences having crowded spikelets; crowded or thick.
Dentate	Coarse, pointed teeth spreading at right angles to the margin.
Denticulate	Small teeth along the margins of an object that are perpendicular to the margin; smaller than dentate.
Diadelphous	Stamen that are divided into two groups by their united filaments.
Diffuse	Open and much branched, widely spread.
Digitate	Parts (three or more) arising from the summit of a structure (e.g., branches of the *Chloris* inflorescence.)
Dilated	Expanded, enlarged, or wider.
Dioecious	Unisexual, the staminate and pistillate flowers being on separate plants.

Disarticulating   Separating at the joints naturally at maturity.
Discoid   Resembling a disk or platter.
Disk flower   Tubular flowers of the Asteraceae head.
Dissected   Deeply divided into numerous parts.
Distichous   Obviously 2-ranked.
Divergent   Extending away from each other by degrees.
Dorsal   Relating to the back of an organ, away from the axis; abaxial surface.
Drupe   Fleshy, indehiscent fruit, usually with a single stony seed (a cherry).
Elliptic   Arching margins of leaf which is pointed at both ends, about two times longer than wide.
Elongate   Narrow, the length several times the width or thickness.
Emarginate   An apex with a shallow notch.
Endosperm   Nutritive tissue near the embryo of the seed; develops from a fusion of polar nuclei and sperm nucleus.
Entire   A continuous margin without teeth or lobes.
Erect   Upright in relation to the ground; perpendicular to the ground.
Exserted   Protruding (e.g., the inflorescence from the sheath.)
Fascicle   Small bundle or cluster.
Fertile   Capable of producing a fruit or caryopsis.
Filiform   Thread-like.
First glume   The lowermost glume, odd-nerved, an empty bract.
Flexuous   Bent gradually in one direction and then another.
Floral axis   The structure to which the palea and flower are attached.
Floret   The lemma, floral axis, and palea with the included flower (pistil, stamen, and lodicules) or caryopsis.
Flowering   Producing the male and female reproductive structures.
Follicle   Dry, dehiscent fruit with one suture, develops from a single carpel.
Forb   Herbaceous plants, excluding grasses and grass-like plants.
Fruit   The ripened ovary.
Funnelform   Widening upwards, like a funnel; a flower form.
Fusiform   Spindle-shaped; widest near the middle and tapering in toward both ends.
Geniculate   Bent sharply, like a bent knee.
Glabrate   Almost glabrous.
Glabrescent   Becoming glabrous (without hairs) as that plant structure ages or matures.
Glabrous   Without hairs or vestiture of any type.
Glandular   Bearing glands.
Glaucous   A waxy bloom or white covering of a surface. In plants the result is usually a bluegreen color.
Globose   Round or spherical.
Glochid   Minute barbed spines in prickly pear cacti; usually in tufts.
Glumes   The pair of bracts at the base of the spikelet, odd-nerved, empty bracts that may be awned or awnless.
Habit   General appearance or aspect of a plant; growth form.
Habitat   Particular site or community of occurrence.

Head   A dense cluster of sessile or subsessile flowers arising from a common area on the peduncle.

Herbaceous   Having the character of an herb; not woody. Grasses, grass-likes, and forbs are herbs.

Hirsute   Covered with coarse, straight rather stiff hairs, usually perpendicular to the surface.

Hispid   Rough with erect, bristly hairs.

Hyaline   Thin and translucent or transparent.

Hypanthium   Cup-like tube derived from the fusion of calyx, corolla, and stamen.

Imbricate   Overlapping, as do shingles on a roof.

Imperfect   Having unisexual flowers. Having either stamen or pistil (carpels) but not both.

Indehiscent   Not opening at maturity, staying closed.

Indurate   Hard.

Infertile   Incapable of sexual reproduction.

Inflated   Puffed up, bladdery.

Inflorescence   The flowering part of a plant, above the uppermost leaf or portion thereof.

Internode   The part of a culm between two successive nodes.

Involucre   A cluster of bristles or sterile branchlets below the spikelets (e.g., in *Cenchrus* and *Pennisetum*).

Involute   Rolled inward from the edges so that the upper surface is within.

Irregular flower Flower with one or more parts of a series of different shape; like zygomorphic.

Joint   The node of a grass culm, spikelet, inflorescence, or any other node.

Keel   The sharp fold at the back of a compressed sheath, glume, lemma, palea, leaf, or caryopsis.

Lacerate   Appearing torn on the margin; irregularly cleft.

Lanate   Woolly covering of short dense hairs.

Lanceolate   Shape or outline like the head of a spear; pointed at both ends and widest below the middle.

Lateral   Referring to the sides.

Latex   A milky sap.

Leaf   The lateral organ of a grass culm, typically consisting of sheath, blade, ligule, and auricles.

Leaflet   A secondary leaf; one part of a compound leaf.

Legume   Fruit of the Fabaceae; dehiscent, dry fruit with one carpel and two sutures.

Lemma   An odd-nerved bract of a spikelet occurring above the glumes; the abaxial bract of the floret that may be awned or awnless.

Lenticels   Corky area (spot) on the bark of many woody stems.

Ligule   The abaxial appendage, a membrane, a ciliate membrane, or a ring of hairs on the inside of a leaf at the junction of sheath and blade; the strap-shaped limb of a ray-flower.

Linear   Long and narrow with parallel margins.

Lobed   A projecting portion of an organ in which the divisions are less than half the distance to the base or midrib; usually rounded at apex.

Locule   Compartment or cell of an ovary, anther, or fruit.

Margins   The edges, e.g., the leaf edge or margins.

Mat-forming A low growth form appearing like a pad.

Membranous Thin, soft, pliable.

Midnerve   The central nerve or vascular bundle of a leaf, lemma, glume, or similar structure.

Midrib   Central vein of a leaf or leaflet.

Monoecious   Having staminate and pistillate flowers on the same plant but each sex on a different flower.

Mucro   A minute awn or excurrent midnerve of an organ (e.g., on a lemma).

Mucronate   Tipped with a short tip or point like an awn. Usually the extension of a nerve beyond the leafy tissue.

Nerve   The vascular bundles or veins or ribs of the blades, glumes, lemmas, and paleas.

Neuter   Without sexual structures; not having stamens or pistils.

Node   The joint of a culm, inflorescence, or spikelet.

Ob-   Prefix meaning inversely.

Oblique   Unequal sides; slanting.

Oblong   Object with round ends and parallel margins, three times longer than wide.

Obovate   Egg-shaped with widest part above the middle.

Obovoid   A solid that is obovate in outline.

Obtuse   Pointed with an angle greater than 90°. A broad pointed apex or base.

Open   Loose, spreading (e.g., inflorescences, with few spikelets and long branches).

Opposite   Structures that are paired at node and one on each side of the node; stamen inserted directly in front of the petal; leaves are also opposite.

Orbicular   Approaching a circular outline.

Oval   Broadly elliptical.

Ovate   Egg-shaped with the widest part below the middle.

Ovoid   A solid that is oval in flat outline.

Ovulate   Bearing ovules.

Ovule   The structure within the ovary that will become the seed after fertilization.

Paired   Occurring in two's, e.g., two spikelets per node.

Palea   The abaxial bract of a floret; two-nerved, arising from the floral axis.

Palmate   Three or more lobes, nerves or leaflets arising from a common point.

Panicle   An inflorescence type in which the central axis branches and rebranches.

Papilionaceous Flower type in much of the Fabaceae; having a banner petal, 2 wing petals, and 2 fused or partially fused keel petals; butterfly-like flower.

Papilla   A minute, nipple-shaped projection.

Papillose   Having minute, nipple-shaped projections on the surface.

Pappus   Scales, hairs, or bristles that crown the summit of the ovary (or achene) in the Asteraceae flower.

Pedicel   The stalk of a spikelet, except for spikelets on a spike inflorescence.

Pedicellate	Having a pedicel.
Peduncle	The stalk or stem of an inflorescence.
Pendulous	Drooping, hanging downward, suspended.
Perennial	Growing more than 2 years; completing several reproductive cycles.
Perfect	Flowers having both stamen and pistils (carpels).
Pericarp	The ripened ovary walls after it becomes a fruit.
Persistent	Remaining attached, either after other parts have been shed or for a considerable period.
Petal	Part or member of the corolla; usually brightly colored or showy.
Petaloid	Petal-like (e.g., a brightly colored leaf or sepal).
Petiole	Stalk of a leaf blade.
Phyllary	Bract of the involucre on the outside of the head of flowers in the Asteraceae.
Pilose	Pubescent with long, soft hairs that are typically straight.
Pinnae	A primary leaflet or division of a pinnately compound leaf.
Pinnate	Having two rows of lateral divisions along the main axis.
Pinnatifid	Cleft, parted, or divided in a pinnate fashion.
Pistillate	Applied to spikelets bearing pistils only and to an inflorescence or a plant with pistillate flowers.
Pitted	Marked with small depressions or pits.
Plumose	Feathery in appearance, having fine hairs on each side.
Podsol	A white or gray soil which is highly leached.
Prickle	Spine-like projection occurring irregularly on the bark or epidermis (e.g., on roses).
Primary branch	Any branch arising from the main axis; all branches that come from the central axis of a grass inflorescence.
Primary unilateral branch	A primary branch with spikelets appearing to develop on one side of the branch.
Prostrate	Lying flat on the ground.
Puberulent	Minutely pubescent.
Pubescent	Covered with short, soft hairs.
Pulvini	A swelling at the base of a leaf or branch of the inflorescence.
Punctate	Covered with glandular dots, pits, or depressions.
Pungent	A sharp point; an acrid taste.
Pyramidal	Triangular in outline; shaped like a pyramid.
Raceme	An inflorescence type in which the spikelets are pedicellate on the rachis.
Racemose	Branches that are like racemes.
Rachilla	The small axis of the spikelet; the structure to which the glumes, lemma and floral axis are attached.
Rachis	The axis of a spike, spicate raceme, or raceme inflorescence; the axis of a compound leaf.
Radiate	Spreading from a common center; bearing rays; flower of the Asteraceae with marginal ray flowers.
Ray flower	Ligulate or strap-shaped flower on the margin of sunflower heads.

Receptacle	Part of the floral axis upon which sepals, petals, stamen, and pistil are borne.
Reduced	Smaller in size, frequently lacking parts; in flowers the sexual parts may be absent.
Reduced floret	A floret that is either staminate or neuter. If it is highly reduced (e.g., awnlike structures) then it is sometimes called a rudimentary floret.
Reflexed	Bend downward or backward.
Resinous	Producing a viscous substance or resin.
Reticulate	In the form of a network like some types of netted venation.
Retrorse	Pointing downward toward the base, as do the barbs on *Cenchrus* (sandbur).
Revolute	Turned under along the margins toward the abaxial surface.
Rhizome	A horizontal, underground stem with modified leaves at the nodes.
Rhizomatous	Having rhizomes.
Rhombic	Nearly diamond-shaped.
Rootstock	Underground stem; rhizome of forbs and woody plants.
Rosette	A cluster of spreading or radiating basal leaves, as in *Dichanthelium*.
Rudiment	An imperfectly developed organ or part, specifically used in reference to florets.
Rudimentary	Not fully developed and non-functional.
Rugose	Wrinkled or folded; having horizontal folds in the surface.
Scabrous	Rough to the touch; caused by short, stiff, angled hairs on the surface.
Scarious	Thin, dry, and membranous; not green (e.g., the margins of a *Poa* lemma).
Schizocarp	Dry, dehiscent fruit that splits into halves such as in the Apiaceae.
Second glume	The uppermost of the two glumes; an odd-nerved, empty bract.
Secondary	Not primary, subordinate; the branches that arise from the primary branches.
Sepal	Part or member of the calyx; usually green but may be petaloid.
Series	Number or group of similar objects arranged in a row.
Serrate	Saw-toothed with the teeth angled toward the apex, sharp teeth.
Sessile	Without a pedicel or stalk or petiole.
Sheath	The lower part of a leaf that encloses the culm; typically split and overlapping at the margins.
Simple	Unbranched as a stem; derived from a single flower or pistil; the leaf with 1 blade.
Sinuate	Having a wavy margin.
Sinus	The recess or space between teeth, lobes, or divisions of a leaf.
Spathe	A modified leaf sheath that subtends and often encloses some of the inflorescence.
Spicate	Spike-like; resembling a spike inflorescence but having both sessile and pedicellate spikelets or flowers.
Spike	An unbranched inflorescence in which the spikelets are sessile on the rachis (main axis).
Spikelet	The basic unit of a grass inflorescence that typically consists of 2 glumes (except in some species where 1 or both glumes are lacking), 1 or more florets, and a rachilla.

Sprout	To initiate growth or germination; give off shoots or buds.
Spines	A sharp pointed, stiff body arising from the epidermis.
Squarrose	Spreading rigidly at right angle; usually the shape of bracts.
Stamen	The male organ of a flower, consisting of the pollen bearing anther on a slender filament. The collective term for stamen is androecium.
Staminate	Containing stamen but not the pistil.
Stellate	Star-shaped; hairs that branch at the base.
Sterile	Without pistils. A sterile floret may be staminate or neuter.
Stigma	The region or area of the gynoecium that is receptive to pollen, usually apical.
Stipule	Appendages (leaf-like, spines, or bracts) usually in pairs at the base of the leaf petiole.
Stolon	A horizontal, above-ground stem with modified leaves.
Stoloniferous	Bearing horizontal above ground stems that root at the nodes.
Striate	Marked with longitudinal grooves or lines; appearing striped.
Strigose	Covered with sharp, stiff, appressed hairs.
Style	Elongated neck of the gynoecium between the ovary and stigma.
Sub-	A prefix used to denote a lesser degree, an inferior rank, or a lower position.
Subtend	To be below and close to; refers to position.
Subulate	Awl-shaped.
Succulent	Fleshy, soft or juicy.
Suffrutescent	Lower plant parts woody, upper stems herbaceous.
Taproot	A large primary root, larger than lateral roots and descending.
Tendril	The twining, climbing organ of a stem or leaf.
Tepal	Part of the perianth not differentiated into calyx and corolla.
Terete	Cylindric and slender, as the normal stems of a grass plant.
Terminal	Borne at or belonging to the extremity or summit; distal.
Thorn	The apex or end of a branch that terminates in a sharp point.
Thyrse	A compact panicle; main axis indeterminate but other axes cymose.
Tiller	An erect, lateral shoot.
Tomentose	A covering of long, dense, tangled hairs.
Toothed	Small, pointed marginal projections.
Triangular	Pyramidal in outline; 3 corners or angles.
Trifoliate	Three leaflets.
Truncate	The apex or base of a structure that is flat or ends abruptly. It appears to be cut off.
Tuberculate	Bearing small projections or warty protuberances.
Tufted	Clustered, caespitose.
Turgid	Swollen or appearing inflated.
Undulate	Wavy in the horizontal plane.
Unilateral	One sided or turned to one side (e.g., the spikelet arrangement on the branches of *Bouteloua*).
Unisexual	Flowers that contain either stamens or pistils but not both.
Verrucose	Covered with warty protuberances.
Verticil	A whorl of parts arising from a common point.
Verticillate	In whorls or verticils at several nodes along an axis.

Vestigal   Imperfectly developed organ.
Vestiture   Surface coverings (e.g., hairs, or wax, or scales).
Villous   Long, soft, unmatted hairs; shaggy.
Viscid   Sticky, glutinous.
Whorl   A cluster of 3 or more branches around the inflorescence axis; 3 or more leaves coming from a single node.
Winged   Bearing a projection or border near the margins that resembles a wing.
Zygomorphic   Bilateral symmetry; only have one plane of dissection which will produce similar halves; having floral parts of different sizes and/or shapes.

SELECTED REFERENCES

Ajilvsgi, G. 1984. Wildflowers of Texas. Shearer Publishing, Bryan, Texas.

Allred, K.W. 1982. Describing the Grass Inflorescence. J. Range Manage. 35(5):672-675.

Barkley, T.M., Editor. 1977. Atlas of the Flora of the Great Plains. Iowa State University Press, Ames.

Beetle, A.A. 1983. Las Gramineas de Mexico. Vol. I. COTECOCA.

Benson, L.D., and R.A. Darrow. 1954. The Trees and Shrubs of Southwestern Deserts. University of New Mexico Press, Albuquerque.

Bentley, H.L. 1898. Grasses and Forage Plants of Central Texas. Bull. 10. Div. Agrostology. United States Dep. Agr., Washington, D.C.

Brown, L. 1985. Grasslands. Albert A. Knopf, Inc. New York.

Copple, R.F., and C.P. Pase. 1967. A Vegetative Key to Some Common Arizona Range Grasses. Res. Paper RM-27. Rocky Mountain Forest and Range Exp. Sta. Forest Service. United States Dep. Agr., Washington, D.C.

Correll, D.S., and H.B. Correll. 1972. Aquatic and Wetland Plants of the Southwestern United States. Environmental Protection Agency, Washington, D.C.

Correll, D.S., and M.C. Johnston. 1970. Manual of the Vascular Plants of Texas. Texas Res. Found., Renner.

Cronquist, A. 1980. Vascular Flora of the Southeastern United States. Vol. 1. Asteraceae. University of North Carolina Press, Chapel Hill.

Cronquist, A., A.H. Holmgren, N.H. Holmgren, J.R. Reveal, and P.K. Holmgren. 1977. Intermountain Flora. Vol. 6. Columbia University Press, New York.

Cronquist, A., A.H. Holmgren, N.H. Holmgren, J.R. Reveal, and P.K. Holmgren. 1984. Intermountain Flora. Vol. 4. Columbia University Press, New York.

Curtis and Curtis, Inc. 1989. Southwest Plants.

Dollahite, J.W., G.R. Housholder, and B.J. Camp. 1966. Oak Poisoning in Livestock. Bull. 1049. Texas Agr. Exp. Sta. Texas A&M University, College Station.

Durrell, L.W., and I.E. Newsom. 1939. Colorado's Poisonous and Injurious Plants. Bull. 455. Agr. Exp. Sta. Colorado State College, Ft. Collins.

Dyksterhuis, E.J. 1948. The Vegetation of the Western Cross Timbers. Ecol. Monogr. 18:325-376.

Elias, T.S. 1980. Trees of North America. Van Nostrand Reinhold Co., New York.

Elmore, F.H. 1976. Shrubs and Trees of the Southwest Uplands. Southwest Parks and Monuments Association, Globe, Arizona.

Evers, R.A., and R.P. Link. 1972. Poisonous Plants of the Midwest and their Effects on Livestock. Spec. Pub. 24. Coll. Agr., University of Illinois, Urbana-Champaign.

Featherly, H.I. 1938. Grasses of Oklahoma. Tech. Bull. 3. Agr. Exp. Sta. Oklahoma Agr. and Mech. College, Stillwater.

Forest Service. 1937. Range Plant Handbook. United States Dep. Agr., Washington, D.C.

Gandhi, K.N., and R.D. Thomas. 1989. Asteraceae of Louisiana. Sida Bot. Misc. No. 4, Dallas.

Gay, C.W., D. Dwyer, C. Allison, S.L. Hatch, and J. Schickedanz. 1980. New Mexico Range Plants. Circ. 374. Coop. Ext. Service. New Mexico State University, Las Cruces.

Gould, F.W. 1951. Grasses of Southwestern United States. Biol. Sci. Bull. No. 7. University of Arizona Press, Tucson.

Gould, F.W., and T.W. Box. 1965. Grasses of the Texas Coastal Bend. Texas A&M University Press, College Station.

Gould, F.W. 1975. The Grasses of Texas. Texas A&M University Press, College Station.

Gould, F.W. 1978. Common Texas Grasses. Texas A&M University Press, College Station.

Gould, F.W., and R.B. Shaw. 1983. Grass Systematics. 2nd Ed. Texas A&M University Press, College Station.

Harrington, H.D. 1954. Manual of the Plants of Colorado. Sage Books, Denver.

Harrington, H.D., and L.W. Durrell. 1957. How to Identify Plants. The Swallow Press Inc., Chicago.

Hatch, S.L., C.W. Morden, and B.W. Woie. 1984. The Grasses of the National Range Research Station, Kiboko (Kenya). MP 1573. Texas Agr. Exp. Sta., College Station.

Hatch, S.L., K.N. Gandhi, and L.E. Brown. 1990. A Checklist of the Vascular Plants of Texas. MP 1655. Texas Agr. Exp. Sta., College Station.

Hermann, F.J. 1966. Notes on Western Range Forbs: Cruciferae through Compositae. United States Dep. Agr., Washington, D.C.

Hignight, K.W., J.K. Wipff, and S.L. Hatch. 1988. Grasses (Poaceae) of the Texas Cross Timbers and Prairies. M.P. 1657. Texas Agr. Exp. Sta., College Station.

Hitchcock, A.S. 1951. Manual of the Grasses of the United States. Revised by Agnes Chase. Misc. Pub. 200. United States Dep. Agr., Washington, D.C.

Jones, F.B. 1975. Flora of the Texas Coastal Bend. Mission Press, Corpus Christi.

Judd, B.I. 1962. Principal Forage Plants of Southwestern Ranges. Sta. Paper 69. Rocky Mountain Forest and Range Exp. Sta. Forest Service. United States Dep. Agr., Washington, D.C.

Kartesz, J.T., and R. Kartesz. 1980. A Synonymized Checklist of the Vascular Flora of the United States, Canada, and Greenland. Vol. II. The biota of North America. University of North Carolina Press, Chapel Hill.

Kearney, T.H., and R.H. Peebles. 1960. Arizona Flora. University of California Press, Berkeley.

Kingsbury, J.M. 1964. Poisonous Plants of the United States and Canada. Prentice-Hall, Inc., Englewood Cliffs, New Jersey.

Leithead, H.L., L.L. Yarlett, and T.N. Shiftlet. 1971. 100 Native Forage Grasses in 11 Southern States. Agr. Handbook 389. Soil Conservation Service. United States Dep. Agr., Washington, D.C.

Little, E.L., Jr. 1971. Atlas of United States Trees. Vol. 1. Conifers and Important Hardwoods. M.P. 1146. United States Dep. Agr., Washington, D.C.

Loughmiller, C., and L. Loughmiller. 1984. Texas Wildflowers. University of Texas Press, Austin.

MacMahon, J.A. 1985. Deserts. Albert A. Knopf, Inc. New York.

Moreno, N.P. 1984. Glosario Botanico Ilustrado. Inst. Nac. de Invest. Xalapa, Veracruz, Mexico.

Muenscher, W.C. 1939. Poisonous Plants of the United States. Macmillan Publ. Co., Inc., New York.

Munz, P.A., and D.D. Keck. 1959. A California Flora. University of California Press, Berkeley.

Nokes, J. 1986. How to Grow Native Plants of Texas and the Southwest. Texas Monthly Press. Austin.

Parks, H.B. 1937. Valuable Plants Native to Texas. Bull. 551. Texas Agr. Ext. Service. College Station.

Phillips Petroleum Company. 1963. Pasture and Range Plants. Phillips Petroleum Co., Bartlesville, Oklahoma.

Powell, A.M. 1988. Trees and Shrubs of Trans-Pecos Texas. Big Bend Natural History Association. Big Bend National Park, Texas.

Shaw, R.B., and J.D. Dodd. 1976. Vegetative Key to the *Compositae* of the Rio Grande Plains of Texas. M.P. 1274. Texas Agr. Exp. Sta., College Station.

Shields, H. 1984. Desert Plants, Recipes and Remedies. Okesa Publications. Tularosa, New Mexico.

Silveus, W.A. 1933. Texas Grasses. Clegg Co., San Antonio.

Smeins, F.E., and R.B. Shaw. 1978. Natural Vegetation of Texas and Adjacent Areas -- 1675-1975 Bibliography. M.P. 1399. Agr. Exp. Sta. Texas A&M University, College Station.

Sperry, O.E., J.W. Dollahite, G.O. Hoffman, and B.J. Camp. 1977. Texas Plants Poisonous to Livestock. Coop. Ext. Service. Texas A&M University, College Station.

Stechman, J.V. 1977. Common Western Range Plants. Vocational Educ. Productions. California Polytechnic State University, San Luis Obispo.

Stubbendieck, J., S.L. Hatch, and K.J. Hirsch. 1986. North American Range Plants. 3rd ed. University of Nebraska Press, Lincoln.

Stubbendieck, J., S.L. Hatch, and K.J. Kjar. 1982. North American Range Plants. 2nd ed. University of Nebraska Press, Lincoln.

Texas Forest Service. 1963. Forest Trees of Texas. Texas Forest Service, College Station.

Tsvelev, N.N. 1984. Grasses of the Soviet Union. Russian Trans. Ser. 8. A.A. Balkema, Rotterdam.

Turner, B.L. 1959. The Legumes of Texas. University of Texas Press, Austin.

Villarreal-Q, J.A. 1983. Malezas de Buenavista Coahuila. Univ. Aut. Agraria "Antonio Narro". Buenavista, Saltillo, Mexico.

Vines, R.A. 1960. Trees, Shrubs and Woody Vines of the Southwest. University of Texas Press, Austin.

Wasser, C.H. 1982. Ecology and Culture of Selected Species Useful in Revegetating Disturbed Lands in the West. Fish and Wildlife Service, U.S. Dept. of Interior, Washington, D.C.

Waterfall, U.T. 1962. Keys to the Flora of Oklahoma. Oklahoma State University Press, Stillwater.

Weiner, M.A. 1980. Earth Medicine-Earth Food. Macmillian Publ. Co., Inc., New York.

Weniger, D. 1984. Cacti of Texas and Neighboring States. University of Texas Press, Austin.

Williams, K. 1977. Eating Wild Plants. Mountain Press Publ. Co., Missoula, Montana.

INDEX